Ruby Sel

The Johnson-Sims Feud

Romeo and Juliet, West Texas Style

Bill O'Neal

Number 9 in the A. C. Greene Series

University of North Texas Press
Denton, Texas

10 9 8 7 6 5 4 3 2 1

Permissions:
University of North Texas Press
1155 Union Circle #311336
Denton, TX 76203-5017

The paper used in this book meets the minimum requirements
of the American National Standard for Permanence of Paper for
Printed Library Materials, z39.48.1984. Binding materials have
been chosen for durability.

Library of Congress Cataloging-in-Publication Data
O'Neal, Bill, 1942-
  The Johnson-Sims feud : Romeo and Juliet, West Texas style / Bill
O'Neal. -- 1st ed.
      p. cm. -- (Number 9 in the A.C. Greene Series.)
  Includes bibliographical references and index.
  ISBN 978-1-57441-290-1 (cloth : alk. paper)
 1. Vendetta--Texas--Scurry County--History--20th century.
2. Ranchers--Texas--Scurry County--Biography. 3. Frontier and
pioneer life--Texas--Scurry County. 4. Family violence--Texas--
History. 5. Scurry County (Tex.)--History--20th century. I. Title. II.
Series: A.C. Greene series ; 9.
  F392.S4O54 2010
  976.4'731--dc22
                          2010008815

The Johnson-Sims Feud: Romeo and Juliet, West Texas Style is Number
9 in the A. C. Greene Series.

For Betty Miller Giddens

Granddaughter of Emmett
and Rocky Higgins Johnson
Great-granddaughter of W. A.
and Nannie Johnson, and of Pink Higgins

Contents

List of Illustrations

Acknowledgments

I first became acquainted with the Johnson-Sims Feud during the late 1990s, while researching a biography of Pink Higgins. Although I wrote about this West Texas conflict in the last chapters of *The Bloody Legacy of Pink Higgins* (Eakin Press, 1999), I wanted to know more about the Johnson and Sims families. As the years passed, I continued to collect material about these two pioneer families and the events of their tragic clash. Eventually I was urged by Ron Chrisman, director of the University of North Texas Press, to produce a book about the Johnson-Sims Feud, as part of the UNT Press exploration of frontier violence in Texas. I am indebted to Ron for his encouragement and editorial direction as I developed this project.

I am similarly indebted to Betty Miller Giddens, descendant of the Johnson and Higgins families, who made enormous contributions to the Pink Higgins biography. But Betty was convinced that more remained to be told. She continued to pursue leads, then sent me copies of various items or suggested that I contact this or that individual. When I began writing this book, Betty was a willing and knowledgeable sounding board. Throughout the development of this project, she has provided indispensable help.

In San Marcos I met and was charmed by Beverly Sims Benson, the sole surviving family member from the feud years. Lively and personable, Beverly shared with me memories of her parents, Ed Sims and Gladys Johnson Sims Hamer, and of her Johnson and Sims grandparents and other relatives. Although most of her family photographs were destroyed in a fire in California, Beverly provided a couple of surviving photos and a Johnson genealogical chart. Beverly's devoted friend, Ronald Murphree, offered welcome assistance during and after our meeting.

My meeting with Beverly was arranged by Harrison Hamer, grandson and namesake of Texas Ranger Harrison Hamer, who was involved in the Johnson-Sims Feud, along with his celebrated brother, Frank Hamer. The younger Harrison Hamer is an expert chronicler of Frank, Harrison, and the other two Hamer brothers who became Rangers. Harrison generously shared his findings and thoughts with me. In 1997, I enjoyed lengthy phone interviews with Frank Hamer Jr. (now deceased), who offered illuminating insights and information about his parents, Frank and Gladys Johnson Sims Hamer.

Samantha Usnick of Amarillo is the granddaughter of Marshall Higgins, great-granddaughter of Judge Cullen Higgins, and great-great-granddaughter of Pink Higgins. A teacher in Amarillo, Sam is an enthusiastic researcher of her family history, and she graciously provided me with documents, stories, and photographs.

Another Higgins descendant, Bob Terry of Roby, absorbed family stories from his father, Pink Terry. Bob spent years collecting evidence and visiting the sites of various events, and he took me to many of those sites and opened his files to me. Dr. John T. Higgins of Lampasas, a great-grandson of Pink Higgins and great-nephew of Judge Cullen Higgins, shared with me the voluminous materials he has collected during meticulous investigations of his family heritage.

In Post I was extended every courtesy by Ed and Anne Sims. Ed is the namesake and nephew of the first victim of the Johnson-Sims Feud, while Anne is an expert genealogist and businesswoman. Ed and Anne opened their home to me, responding to countless questions and pulling out family photos and artifacts by the score. Ed described and reflected upon his Sims elders, while Anne made numerous arrangements for my visits to Post. Their efforts on my behalf were crucial to my understanding of the Johnsons, and my debt to them is deep.

Also in Post, Gene and Wyvonne Kennedy welcomed me to their home, described Gene's uncle, Will Luman, and escorted me to the cemetery to locate significant gravesites. When I traveled to the still remote headquarters of the former Sims ranch, a property now owned by Dr. Mark D'Alise of Amarillo, I was greeted by foreman Larry Rapier. Larry toured me through every room of the old ranch house, showed me other buildings on the site, and described topographical aspects of the ranch. A bachelor cowboy of the old school, Larry would have fit comfortably into this rugged ranch country a century ago and more.

I was conducted on a tour of the former Johnson ranch by Billy Bob McMullan, who has ranched portions of the old property throughout his life. The son of Helen Trix Sims, Billy Bob is the grandson of Ed Sims and Gladys Johnson Sims Hamer, while his great-grandparents include W. A. and Nannie Johnson and Dave and Laura Belle Sims. He is descended from both feuding families, and is steeped in the background of his ancestors. Billy Bob brought me to every landmark of the great old ranch, while patiently answering all of my questions. Later he provided me with a photo of his mother, and responded to more questions. I am deeply grateful to this admirable West Texan.

Terri Laurence, Assistant Clerk of Garza County, and Craig Harrison, Clerk of Kent County, helped me find particulars about the demise of Dave Sims. At the Callahan County Courthouse in Baird, my search for trial documents was courteously facilitated by District Clerk Cubelle L. Harris and her deputy, Georgie Manion. At the Dawson County Courthouse in Lamesa, Deputy District Clerk Julie Vera cheerfully hunted trial information for me.

Research specialist Kim Smith, of the Southwestern Cattle Raisers Association, aided me in searching for material on stock detective Will Luman. Librarian/archivist Christina Stopka expertly guided me through the holdings of the Texas Ranger Hall of Fame in Waco, while the research staff at the Ector County Library in Odessa produced obscure information about Gee McMeans.

I was enlightened about Elizabethan tragedies in general and *Romeo and Juliet* in particular by one of my daughters, Dr. Shellie O'Neal, chair of the drama department of Navarro College. Another daughter, Dr. Berri O'Neal Gormley, director of the Universities

Center at Dallas, obtained several photographs for me at Snyder's Scurry County Museum.

Berri was aided at the museum by curator Sue Goodwin, who also extended her kind assistance to me on a later visit to this excellent facility. Over lunch I was privileged to query Snyder's superb local historian, Aline Parks. At the Pioneer Museum in Sweetwater I was helped by Annette Mills, who entrusted me to copy and return photographs from the museum's impressive collection.

Two excellent historians from Caldwell County, Chuck and Pat Parsons, took time from their own projects to research Billy Johnson's family background in Gonzales County. I am indebted to them for the fund of material they unearthed. Another author and friend, Dr. Lewis Toland, of the English faculty of the New Mexico Military Institute, placed me in touch with Registrar Ed Preble and Alumni Director Renee James-Bressen, who resourcefully located information about the matriculation of Emmett and Sidney Johnson to NMMI more than a century ago. One of the founding members of the Scurry County Historical Society, Charles G. Anderson, Sr., of Abilene, graciously permitted me to use his wedding photo of Ed and Gladys Sims, the book's most important illustration.

My youngest daughter and her husband, Causby and Dusty Henderson, researched in the Southern Methodist University Library and the Dallas County Courthouse on my behalf, while efficiently converting my handwritten pages to disk. I could not have completed this project without their able assistance. My brother-in-law, John Smith of Lampasas, is a competent genealogist, and he helped me track down information about several people in this book.

Donaly Brice, Research Specialist at the Texas State Library and Archives in Austin, read the manuscript with a meticulous eye for detail. Professor T. Lindsay Baker, W. K. Gordon Endowed Chair in History at Tarleton State University in Stephenville and an accomplished author, also carefully read the manuscript. These two noted Texas historians offered valuable suggestions for improvement and detected errors, and the manuscript was greatly refined by their expertise.

For more than a decade my wife, Karon, has helped me piece together this story. She accompanied me on research trips, worked with me at various research centers, photographed relevant sites, and helped copy numerous old photos. I cannot imagine producing a book without Karon's cheerful and competent collaboration.

Johnson-Sims Country

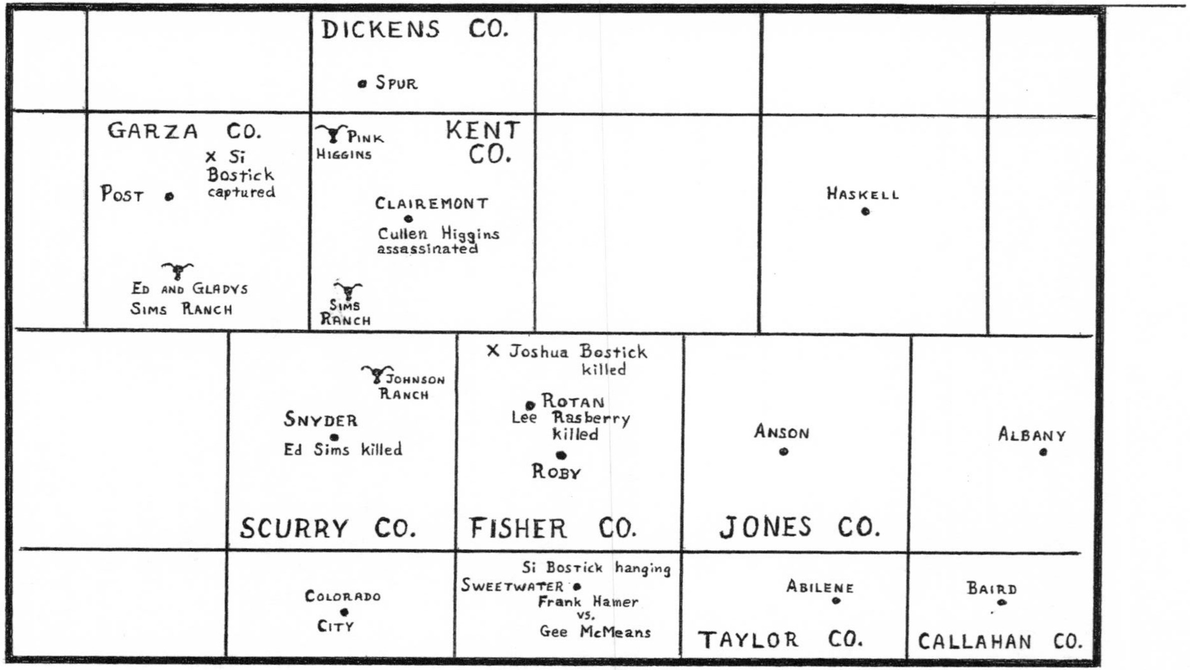

DICKENS CO.

• SPUR

KENT CO.

HASKELL •

CLAIREMONT
Cullen Higgins
assassinated

Y PINK HIGGINS

GARZA CO.
x Si Bostick captured

POST •

ED AND GLADYS SIMS RANCH

SIMS RANCH

JOHNSON RANCH

SNYDER •
Ed Sims killed

X Joshua Bostick killed

• ROTAN
Lee Rasberry killed

ROBY •

ANSON •

ALBANY •

JONES CO.

SCURRY CO.

FISHER CO.

COLORADO • CITY

Si Bostick hanging

SWEETWATER •
Frank Hamer
vs.
Gee McMeans

ABILENE •

BAIRD •

TAYLOR CO.

CALLAHAN CO.

Chapter 1

Introduction to a Blood Feud

"'Vengeance is Mine!' saith the Lord. But in and out of Texas he has always had plenty of help."

C. L. Sonnichsen

There was bad blood between W. A. Johnson and Ed Sims. Johnson was a pioneer cattleman of Scurry County, and as president of Snyder's First National Bank he was a prominent citizen of the community. Sims, the oldest son of another pioneer ranching clan, had married Johnson's headstrong daughter, Gladys, in 1905 when she was fourteen.

The marriage between Ed Sims and Gladys Johnson seemed to signal the union of two successful ranching families. But while two baby girls were born to the young couple, the marriage proved stormy. Ed and Gladys both were proud and hot-tempered. Ed drank heavily, and each spouse accused the other of extramarital romances. Amid charges and countercharges, Ed and Gladys divorced in 1916.

During the bitter aftermath of divorce, Ed became convinced that the Johnsons were trying to turn his daughters against him. On Friday evening, December 15, 1916, Ed came to Snyder so that he could pick up the girls the next day for a prearranged custody visit. Encountering his former father-in-law in a drugstore that evening, Ed brandished a revolver while vehemently accusing the entire Johnson family of attempting to alienate his daughters against him.

When W. A. Johnson returned to his luxurious ranch house later that night, he related the incident to family members. Gladys and her volatile brother, Sidney, were infuriated. The next day at noon, when Gladys reluctantly drove her little girls into town, she brought her automatic pistol. W. A. Johnson had taught his children to shoot, and more than once Gladys had proved willing to go to her gun.

In Snyder, both the county sheriff and city marshal were on the alert for trouble when Gladys arrived in town. She parked near her father's bank, and Ed walked over to kiss his daughters and take their suitcases. But the girls were upset and crying, and Gladys snapped. She produced her automatic and opened fire. Four shots rang out, and Ed staggered away from the car.

While astounded Saturday shoppers looked to the sound of gunfire, Billy Johnson charged out of the bank to protect his grand-daughters. And Sidney Johnson suddenly emerged onto the sidewalk clutching his shotgun. As Ed stumbled away from the car, the shotgun roared . . .[1]

The shooting in Snyder triggered the last blood feud in Texas. The Johnson-Sims Feud featured traditional elements of the murderous conflicts that had embroiled Texans for three-quarters of a century. The first Texas feud was the Regulator-Moderator War that wracked East Texas with homicidal violence from 1840 through 1844. More than thirty men were killed in assassinations, lynchings, ambushes, street fights, and pitched battles. The sheriff of Harrison County was murdered, and so was Judge John M. Hansford. Senator Robert Potter, a signer of the Texas Declaration of Independence, was slain by Regulators. Courts ceased to operate and anarchy reigned in Shelby County, the Panola District, and Harrison County. Only the personal intervention of President Sam Houston and an invasion of Shelby County by 600 members of the militia of the Republic of Texas halted the bloodletting.[2]

Ed Sims, the first victim of the last blood feud in Texas. *Courtesy Ed and Anne Sims.*

The backwoods warriors of frontier East Texas established for future feudists an imposing standard of murderous violence, as well as for deeds of heroism, endurance, and sheer physical courage. But two decades passed before feuding again broke out in Texas. During the poisonous atmosphere of Reconstruction, the Early-Hasley Feud pitted former Confederates against Union supporters in Bell County, where sporadic violence erupted from 1865 until 1869. The same causes triggered the vicious Lee-Peacock Feud, 1867–1871.[3]

The turbulence of post-Civil War Texas provided a fertile breeding ground for a vast crime ring of rustlers, thieves, and murderers headed by the Taylor clan. Among the lawmen who opposed the Taylors was Bill Sutton, who was murdered in front of his young wife and child in 1874. There were rumors that earlier generations of Taylors and Suttons had clashed in the Carolinas and Georgia. Fighting alongside the Taylors was the notorious killer John Wesley Hardin, who shot Sheriff Jack Helm to death in 1873. Ambushes and street fights of the 1860s and 1870s produced numerous victims.[4]

Texas was rife with lawlessness during the 1870s, and feuding was at its height. The Horrell-Higgins Feud in Lampasas County pitted the Horrell brothers, who were rustlers and chronic troublemakers, against rancher-gunman Pink Higgins and his followers. Higgins killed one of the Horrell brothers in a Lampasas saloon, two other brothers were lynched, and there was violence in and around town. The Hoo Doo War, or Mason County War, was essentially a violent clash between Anglo- and German-Americans, with the murderous conflict aggravated by cattle theft.[5]

Lynching feuds in Shackelford County and in Bastrop County during the troubled 1870s featured extralegal hangings triggered by cattle rustling and highway robberies and retributions. Vigilante justice in Bastrop County was aimed at a gang of thieves, with hangings continuing into the 1880s. In Hood County the Mitchell and Truitt families feuded in 1874 over a land dispute, and two of the Truitts were wounded fatally. The next year Cooney Mitchell was hanged legally in Granbury. Cooney's son, Bill Mitchell, blamed the Reverend James

Truitt, a young minister whose testimony was a key to the
After nursing his grudge for more than a decade, Bill a:
Reverend Truitt in his home in Timpson in 1886. Over a q
century later, the elusive Mitchell finally was imprisoned, but within
two years he escaped.[6]

The Jaybird-Woodpecker War of Fort Bend County originated
with efforts to control the voting of former slaves, before spread-
ing to include feuding families. The sheriff was killed during a wild
shootout in front of the courthouse in 1889. At the turn of the century, feuding returned to the edge of Regulator-Moderator country.
The Wall-Border-Broocks Feud exploded in San Augustine in 1900.
Curg Border, a relative of the influential Broocks family, killed Sheriff
George Wall, an old enemy, in the streets of San Augustine. Eugene
Wall killed Ben Broocks in retaliation, followed by a gun battle around
the courthouse in which two more men were slain. Court action produced no convictions, but rough justice was meted out through a series
of shootings, climaxing with the death of Curg Border at the hands of
a new sheriff.[7]

Early in his long and productive tenure at the Texas College of
Mines and Metallurgy in El Paso (the institution later became Texas
Western College, then the University of Texas at El Paso), Dr. C. L.
Sonnichsen became fascinated by blood feuds. A native of Iowa with
a Ph.D. from Harvard, the young scholar came to Texas and was captivated by the tales of deadly feuds in the Lone Star State. Terming
himself a "feud collector," during the 1930s and 1940s Doc Sonnichsen avidly researched feuding in Texas. Eventually he published two
classic volumes on the subject, *I'll Die Before I'll Run: The Story of the
Great Feuds of Texas* (1951) and *Ten Texas Feuds* (1957). Sonnichsen
became convinced that "the feud is one of the oldest of human institutions [and] one of the hardest to get rid of . . . ." He offered a definition
of a feud: "Any prolonged quarrel involving blood vengeance between
families or factions." He emphasized that "family loyalties almost
always run up the temperature." This emphasis certainly was embodied by the Johnson-Sims conflict.[8]

Sonnichsen reflected upon "the instinct for getting even" and upon "the oldest code known to man—the law of private vengeance." If frontier legal systems did not provide justice, Texans often embraced "folk justice." Frontier Texas thus resorted "to an appeal to a law that is felt to be a reasonable substitute for legal redress which cannot be obtained—sometimes to a law that is higher or more valid than those on the statute books."

Sonnichsen became convinced that feuds rarely broke out "among the rebellious and unrestrained, but among highly conservative people who cling to their ancient followings. Strictly speaking, such people are not lawless—they are just operating under an earlier and more primitive code." Among Texans "the folk law of the frontier was reinforced by the unwritten laws of the South and produced a habit of self-redress more deeply ingrained perhaps than anywhere else in the country."

It was natural for families or factions in conflict to go to their guns because the habit of frontier violence became instilled in Texans. While most states endured frontier conditions for only a decade or so, in Texas the frontier period lasted for most of the nineteenth century. Red and white Texans grappled in a life-and-death struggle for decades, until the 1880s. A study of western clashes between Indians and white men revealed that Texas led all states and territories as the site of known fights with at least 846, while Arizona, the next most troubled area in this regard, was the scene of just over 400 Indian combats. Sixty-one Congressional Medals of Honor were awarded to United States soldiers who served in Texas after the Civil War.[9]

During the 1840s Texas Rangers used the newly invented Colt revolving pistol during horseback fights against Comanche warriors. The revolver was refined and popularized as a weapon in Texas, and by the 1850s Texans were blazing away at each other in gunfights with six-shooters. A survey of 255 western gunfighters and 589 shootouts involving these men revealed that Texas dominated the action of frontier pistoleers. More gunfights—nearly 160—occurred in Texas than in any other state or territory. No other western commonwealth was the arena of even half this many shootings between professional—or habitual—gunfighters. Most western states and territories saw widespread gunfighting activity for only a short number of years before law and order prevailed: Kansas, for example, during the cattle town era; New Mexico during the bloody Lincoln County War; and Oklahoma during its lawless heyday as a refuge for outlaws. But gunfighters became active in Texas during the 1850s and continued their life and death encounters until past the turn of the century.[10]

More frontier gunfighters were born in Texas than in any other state or territory, and more died in Texas than in any other state. Texas produced prominent gunfighters, from the psychopathic John Wesley Hardin to the West's premier assassin, Killin' Jim Miller. There was famed Texas Ranger John R. Hughes, deadly outlaw-lawman King Fisher, and John Selman, who numbered Wes Hardin and ex-Texas Ranger Baz Outlaw among his victims. Eleven of Ben Thompson's fourteen gunfights were in Texas. Doc Holliday fought the first of his eight gunfights in Dallas in 1875, and the following year Bat Masterson engaged in his inaugural shootout in a Mobeetie saloon. Henry Brown killed the first of his five career victims in a Panhandle cattle camp in 1876. Ben Thompson, Wes Hardin, John Selman, Baz Outlaw, King Fisher, Sam Bass, Dallas Stoudenmire, and "Longhair" Jim Courtright are among the noted western gunfighters who met their ends in Texas shootouts.

Texas gunfighters continued their lethal activities into the twentieth century. Pink Higgins, who had used his guns against Comanche warriors, stock thieves, and personal adversaries since he was a teenager, clashed with fellow range detective Bill Standifer in 1902. Although now in his fifties, Pink rode out to meet Standifer in a *mano a mano* rifle duel. Pink drilled Standifer, who was buried on the open range where he died. Killin' Jim Miller, headquartering in Fort Worth, murdered one victim after another until he was lynched in 1909.

Texas feudist Pink Higgins. During the Horrell–
Higgins War, Pink killed one Horrell brother, and
may have helped lynch two others. From a cracked
tintype. Courtesy Betty M. Giddens.

As the conflict between the Johnson and Sims families proved, even in the second decade of the twentieth century West Texans continued to embrace the values and attitudes of the frontier. West Texans still bristled with the violent impulses of the pioneers who had settled the region only a generation earlier.

In addition to the lethal traditions of West Texas of the recent past, the Johnson and Sims feudists shared similarities with one of the most popular and famous Elizabethan tragedies, William Shakespeare's *Romeo and Juliet*. Written (1594–95) and first staged (1597) more than three centuries before the Johnson-Sims Feud, *Romeo and Juliet* would find a real-life interpretation in West Texas during the second decade of the twentieth century.

"Two households, both alike in dignity," begins the prologue to the famous play, "in fair Verona, where we lay our scene . . . ." The scene for the Johnson-Sims conflict was Snyder and Post City, Sweetwater and Clairemont, as well as the harsh rangelands of the surrounding countryside. Like the two households of Verona, both successful ranch households had dignity, as well as pride and courage and a strong sense of family honor.

Romeo and Juliet were proclaimed "a pair of star-cross'd lovers," a description that perfectly fit Ed and Gladys. Gladys was just fourteen when she married, while Juliet was in her fourteenth year. Although Romeo also was a teenager, Ed was twenty-one. But if he had known the disastrous direction his marriage would take, Ed surely would have echoed the words of Romeo: "O, I am fortune's fool."[11]

Conflict is necessary to produce tragedy, and Shakespeare could lay one conflict atop another: man versus man, man versus himself, man versus nature, man versus society. The Johnson and Sims families, and their partisans, resonated with these conflicts. Shakespeare was a master of subplots and, like *Romeo and Juliet*, the Johnson-Sims Feud was a maze of subplots.

While he was dying in Verona, Mercutio bitterly gasped, "A plague o' both your houses."[12] The Capulets and Montagues suffered the plague of heartbreaking losses, but by play's end redemption was achieved through the reconciliation of the feuding families. In West Texas there would be no such reconciliation, although redemption would be attained in another way.

The tale of the Johnson-Sims Feud began with two pioneer ranching families who were determined to create cattle empires in the rugged vastness of West Texas.

Chapter 2

Billy Johnson, Cattle Baron

"I was on an easy fox-trotting bay gelding riding point on a mixed herd of South Texas cattle . . . when I heard the sweet sound of running water as my horse broke stride to jump the creek."

Billy Johnson, cowboy

By the time that pioneer cattlemen Billy Johnson and Dave Sims arrived in West Texas, Americans had become captivated by the range cattle industry. This fascinating enterprise evolved in Texas during the nineteenth century. Cattle were introduced to the Western hemisphere in the early 1500s by Spanish colonizers. On the ranges of northern Mexico, *vaqueros* handled cattle from horseback, developing special attire, techniques, and equipment. Roping, branding, heavy-duty saddles, wide brimmed *sombreros*, high-heeled boots, jingling spurs, leather *chaparejos*—everything had utilitarian purposes, but came to seem colorful and even romantic.

Through the centuries cattle strayed into the brush country above the Rio Grande, multiplying freely in a harsh, unpopulated land. The animals became hardy survivors, good at finding water and forage, and aggressive against predators, fighting with horns that evolved into long, dangerous weapons. During the mid-1800s, Anglo Texans adapted the techniques and equipment of the *vaqueros*, and began trailing herds of rugged "longhorns" to distant markets such as California and New Orleans. But before these long drives could become a regular activity, the Civil War blocked Texas from almost all cattle markets, while most able-bodied men served with the Confederate Army or the home guard.

Unattended and ignored, longhorn cattle multiplied prolifically. By war's end as many as five million wild longhorns ranged across the grasslands of Texas, while a hungry market for beef opened in the industrial Northeast. Longhorns costing no more than three or four dollars in Texas would bring thirty to fifty dollars in northern markets. Herds of half-wild cattle were rounded up by Texas "cow boys" and driven toward the nearest railroads, first to Missouri along the Sedalia Trail, then to Kansas along the Chisholm Trail and the Great Western Trail.

There was much to admire about young drovers. On the long drives cowboys faced stampedes, treacherous river crossings, and other perils. Longhorns were big, ornery beasts, dangerous to both men and horses, and cowboys had to ride and rope with athletic skill to handle these challenging creatures. Booted and spurred, clad in big hats and chaps and bright bandannas, cowboys relished the majestic feeling of power and height and superiority of mounted men throughout history. For cowboys the rollicking climax to the long drives was arrival at Abilene or Dodge City or other railroad towns.

The flamboyant combination of dangerous frontier journeys and brave, colorful cowboys created a romantic adventure that would prove unforgettable to the American public. In the ringing prose of Texas historian T. R. Fehrenbach, the range cattle industry "burned its image like a smoking cattle brand into the consciousness not only of North America but the entire world." He emphasized that Texas cattlemen and cowboys conducted their picturesque venture "with a barbaric magnificence equaled nowhere. They exploded not a business, but a new way of life, across the entire North American West."

Interior of the First National Bank, with President Billy Johnson standing in front, wearing a bow tie and holding his big rancher's hat. Courtesy Scurry County Museum, Snyder, Texas.

Another distinguished Texas historian, Joe B. Frantz, wrote extensively about cattlemen and cowboys and longhorns, concluding that "the range-cattle era placed an indelible stamp on the American character that transcends Texas, the West, and the frontier."[1]

Fehrenbach reflected deeply about cattlemen, finding that "something in its way of life called strongly to certain breeds of men . . . ." Responding to this powerful call were men like Billy Johnson and Dave Sims, in addition to legendary cattlemen such as Charles Goodnight. "A Charles Goodnight could move early onto the far edge of nowhere, and hold his new range against all comers. Some men could not."[2] Billy Johnson could, and so could Dave Sims.

Billy Johnson discovered his "new range" in 1878, just two years after Goodnight founded his famous JA ranch in Palo Duro Canyon. Johnson would put together a ranch of forty-seven contiguous deeded sections, and a decade later Dave Sims would assemble forty sections. Their ranches would comprise more than 30,000 and 25,000 acres respectively and stretch for several miles in each direction.

But by the mid-1880s Goodnight, with the backing of British financier John Adair, ran more than 100,000 JA cattle on 1,335,000 acres. The first great Texas ranch was founded in the mid-1850s by Richard King, a tough visionary who battled vicious enemies and forbidding elements to carve out a legendary empire. By the turn of the century, 75,000 cattle, along with 10,000 horses and mules, grazed on 1,150,000 King Ranch acres in South Texas. Shanghai Pierce organized El Rancho Grande in 1865, combating rustlers with deadly force while branding as many as 18,000 calves a year. John Chisum established his first ranch north of Fort Worth during the 1850s, fighting Comanche raiders and cattle rustlers. But during the Civil War Chisum moved his operations to West Texas, and after the war he drove his cattle into New Mexico. By 1875 at least 80,000 "Jinglebobs" (Chisum's cattle were nicknamed after his famous earmark) were scattered across a vast range, easy targets for rustlers. Chisum employed as many as 100 riders, many of whom were better gunmen than cowboys, and he often led his men in pursuit of stock thieves.

Chisum was called the "Cattle King of the Pecos." Charles Goodnight also was a cattle king, and so were Shanghai Pierce and Richard King. Pioneer cattle kings in other states included John Wesley Iliff and John Wesley Prowers of Colorado; F. E. Warren, Moreton Frewen, Ora Haley, Alexander Swan, and John Kendrick—a native Texan—of Wyoming; Henry Hooker of Arizona; Henry Miller of California; and Honest John Sparks—another native Texan with a blood connection to the Johnson-Sims Feud—of Nevada.

These cattle kings reigned over a vast expanse of wild, magnificent rangelands, accumulating colossal herds of cattle and maintaining their property through courage, hard work, and sheer force of character. These powerful ranchers proudly ran their cattle kingdoms like feudal nobles, with brands and ear marks their heraldry, hard-riding cowboys their knights, and roundups their tournaments.

This medieval analogy should include "cattle baron," a term often used interchangeably with "cattle king." But a medieval king ruled over a great area, commanding a large force of knights, while a baron was "a member of the lowest rank of nobility," according to Webster. The baron ruled over a more modest principality, with a smaller number of knights—and he was included as a member of the nobility, even if outranked by kings and princes.

Although their holdings never reached the enormity of such cattle kings as Charles Goodnight, Richard King, Shanghai Pierce, and John Chisum, Billy Johnson and Dave Sims at least were lords of substantial domains. Johnson and Sims each built and held ranches exceeding 25,000 acres in a hard land. In cattle country Johnson and Sims were ranchers of tangible status, elevated well above a four-section settler with a handful of cows and no employees.

Billy Johnson grew up in the cattle culture, the son of Gonzales County rancher A. B. Johnson, from Mississippi. When Billy was an eight-year-old boy, his father hired a young cowboy named R. T.

Mellard. "Fortunately for me I met and worked for A. B. Johnson," reminisced Mellard, "one of the finest men I ever knew."[3]

A.B. Johnson married a widow, Caroline Wilson, who brought four daughters to the marriage. In 1862 the couple had a son, William A., and during the next eight years two more children were born, Ida and Albert Sidney. A. B. Johnson and his family lived on their land near Wrightsboro, about ten miles southwest of the historic town of Gonzales. He served the public as a justice of the peace, and acquired a term of respect. "Judge A. B. Johnson is in town and stated his 18 foot water well is 'the best in Texas' . . . ," remarked the *Gonzales Inquirer*. But Judge Johnson's principal activity was a stock raiser, and his cattle were branded XV.[4]

Like all boys raised on a ranch, Billy and Sidney learned to ride at an early age. Texas boys were taught to shoot, and on ranches youngsters learned roping, branding, and other skills needed for handling livestock. Billy Johnson was only four when the long drives to northern railheads began. While Texas cowboys became colorful heroes in the public imagination, Billy was making a hand on his father's ranch. He was bright and energetic, and he learned about cattle and cowboying from the back of a cow pony.

Gonzales County was one of the original Texas counties, the site of the first battle of the Texas Revolution and a center of early Anglo settlement. With rich soils and "an unfailing supply of water," farmers produced great amounts of corn and cotton, along with a variety of other agricultural products. But cattle thrived on the nutritious grasses, and many farmers also were stock raisers. There were nearly 30,000 head of cattle in Gonzales County by 1853, and the county's first two cattle drives were organized that year, with herds of 500 and 600. After the Civil War cattle were driven by the thousands toward the Chisholm Trail, and by 1870 more than 75,000 head were being raised in Gonzales County. All of these cattle were tempting targets for stock thieves, especially members of the Taylor outlaw ring. [5]

Like any young cowboy of the era, Billy Johnson longed for the adventure of a trail drive. Since 1871 Crawford Burnett of Gonzales

Pioneer cattleman W. A. "Billy" Johnson, who
established one of the first ranches in isolated
Scurry County in 1878. Courtesy Betty M.
Giddens.

County had contracted with Armour and Company to deliver multiple herds of steers to Chicago buyers in Kansas. Every year Burnett would put together vast herds in the Hill Country, sending them up the trail in bands of 1,000, with a crew and chuck wagon, while continuing to gather more cattle for the next drive and the next. R. T. Mellard, who married W. A. Johnson's stepsister, Sallie, hired on with Burnett in 1871 and was a trail boss for nearly two decades.[6]

When Billy Johnson was sixteen he had the opportunity to join one of the trail drives originating in Gonzales County, and some of the cattle wore Billy's brand. Either through the advice or example—or both—of his father, Billy intended to run his own cattle on his own land. In the cattle boom decade of the 1870s, ranchers were admired and respected. Even at sixteen, Billy Johnson aimed to join the ranks of these powerful men. He took part, or perhaps all, of his wages in cattle, and when a trail drive was organized in 1878, Billy added cattle of his own. A larger herd was organized in Burnet County, where Billy Johnson made fast friendships.

From Burnet County the herd angled northwest, apparently headed toward a market in gold-rich Colorado. Grazing on spring grass, the cattle were driven slowly along the Colorado River, then north toward the Double Fork of the Brazos River. On a warm day in May, ambitious young Billy Johnson was riding point in unsettled country in newly created Scurry County when he experienced an epiphany. Impulsively he decided to build a ranch on the well-watered, broken rangeland in front of him. He never tired of telling the story to his family.

"I was on an easy fox-trotting bay gelding riding point on a mixed herd of South Texas cattle up the trail north and west from Burnet County—we had followed the Colorado River, then cut across the breaks toward Double Mountain—the cattle were in good shape on grass stirrup high, but the day was hot for the middle of May—when I heard the sweet sound of running water as my horse broke stride to jump the creek."[7]

The stirrup-high grass was bluestem, and native grasses of lesser height included sideoats grama, switch grass, and buffalo grass. Scattered trees included cottonwoods, willows, cedars, hackberries, chinaberries, and elms. There were wild grapes and plums. Wildlife included antelopes, deer, wolves, coyotes, wildcats, rabbits, and prairie dogs. Less desirable elements of the countryside were rattlesnakes and cactus; mesquite trees had not yet reached the region.

Comanches and buffaloes only recently had vanished from Scurry County. During the Red River War of 1874–75, a methodical military sweep drove Comanches and Kiowas onto their reservations in southwestern Indian Territory. Buffalo hunters, led by the noted J. Wright Mooar, entered Scurry County in the fall of 1876. On his first morning Mooar sighted, then shot and skinned, a rare white buffalo. Mooar kept more than a dozen skinners busy, and other hunters came with their skinners.

By 1877 Tucker Cornelius, W. H. "Pete" Snyder, and a few other pioneer merchants were trading with hide hunters from "Hidetown," a tiny cluster of dugouts and half-dugouts along the banks of Rough Creek near the center of Scurry County. The isolated hamlet attracted enough frontier riffraff for "Hidetown" also to be called "Robber's Roost" and "Scab Town." Because of Pete Snyder's trading post the village began to be known as "Snyder's Place" and, eventually, "Snyder."[8]

Buffaloes soon were hunted out of the county, and J. Wright Mooar and his brother, John, began running a few cattle on the open range. Another pair of brothers, Tom and Jim Nunn, brought a herd of cattle into the county in October 1877. "The only settlers here then," related Jim Nunn, "were buffalo hunters and supply people—nothing here but grass, prairie dogs, buffalo, coyotes, lobo wolves, and some wildcats and bear."[9]

Several months later, in May 1878, Billy Johnson rode across Ennis Creek on his bay gelding. Captivated by the sweeping grasslands in every direction, he cut out a few head of his cows and calves

Rancher Billy Bob McMullan, great-grandson of Billy Johnson, standing above Ennis Creek. The spring-fed creek attracted young Johnson in 1878, and has never gone dry. Photo by the author.

and left them to graze near the creek. Within months the determined young cowboy returned to the country that had cast a spell over him. He erected a half dugout near a spring on Ennis Creek, heightening the underground structure with a few feet of rock walls. Most dugouts in early Snyder County had hide roofs, and were magnets for rattlesnakes and centipedes and other unwelcome visitors.

Like other ranchers on the edge of the frontier, Billy Johnson pre-empted grazing land. Indeed, Texas required a minimum age of eighteen for purchasers of state land, so Johnson would have to wait until 1880 to submit "an application in waiting" to the General Land Office. Because Texas had been an independent republic, the unique Treaty of Annexation in 1845 permitted the Lone Star State to retain control of its public lands. The federal government controlled public lands in all other states and territories, but Texas was free to sell or allot tens of millions of acres of unsettled land.

The so-called "Fifty Cent Law" of 1879 permitted the purchase of unappropriated land in any quantity for fifty cents an acre. Speculators and ranchers bought great amounts of this land, but the Fifty Cent Law depressed the prices of privately owned lands, in some areas to as low as fifteen cents per acre.

When ambitious young Billy Johnson arrived in West Texas, land was cheap and easy to acquire. He understood that it was imperative to abandon pre-emption and purchase his own land. Just as Richard King built his legendary ranch by methodically obtaining title to one parcel after another, Billy Johnson would carefully piece together his own large property. Through the years he would instill the principle of land acquisition into his family. Long after his death, his grandson Weldon Johnson emphatically remembered: "One thing we have learned—Never sell a dime, not an ounce of land. Never!"[10]

Exhilarated by the wide-open, unclaimed grasslands of Scurry County, Billy Johnson returned to his family home and to Burnet County. With missionary zeal he told friends and family about the expansive new land on the northwestern Texas frontier. Johnson's pioneer fervor was infectious.

For more than two centuries westering men had returned home and enthusiastically advertised new country on the American frontier, and always they had been followed by other men restless with the desire to see a primeval region. Burnet County only recently had been a frontier, and men—and women—from the county soon followed Johnson and each other to this new frontier.

T. J. Faught and O. P. "Pack" Wolf came from Burnet County with their wives, Ophelia Sims Faught and Mollie Sims Wolf. Faught built a dugout, like almost everyone else in Scurry County, but soon erected a two-room rock house. The Faught home was near Rough Creek, and O. P. and Mollie Sims Wolf settled close by. W. D. "Billy" Sims, younger brother of Ophelia and Mollie, came out from Burnet County, established bachelor quarters near Dripping Springs, and began building a substantial ranch. Sidney Johnson later followed his older brother to the area, although he settled to the north in Kent County. [11]

A trio of Smith brothers, George, Jack, and Lon—whose sister would marry Dave Sims—drove cattle from Burnet County, grazing their herd in what would become Kent County, before settling in Scurry County. They soon were joined by R. T. Mellard, who had cowboyed for A. B. Johnson and married his stepdaughter—and Billy's stepsister— Sallie Wilson. Mellard related that in 1879, he and three partners "pooled our cattle and started our herd to Albany in Shackelford County where I cut my cattle, the range not being good, and drove them west. . . . In the fall of 1880 I turned them over to my wife's half-brother, W. A. Johnson, on shares for a period of five years."[12]

Meanwhile, Billy Johnson earned wages and livestock by riding on cattle drives, including one in the employ of Dan and Tom Waggoner to the Kansas City Stock Yards. The Census of 1880 listed Billy, not in Scurry County, but at the Gonzales County home of his parents, working as a "farmer." But this farmer turned eighteen in 1880, old enough to file for the section of land on which he had built his half-dugout, Section 238, Block 2, Houston and Texas Central Railroad Survey.[13]

Over 32 million acres of Texas public lands—the approximate size of Alabama—had been granted to more than forty railroad companies to stimulate the construction of rail lines across the Lone Star State. Some of these companies went bankrupt and their lands were sold for a few cents an acre, but by 1890 Texas had more than 8,700 miles of track.

Unfortunately, no railroad would reach Scurry County until the twentieth century. While Scurry County was being developed, the nearest railroad was the Southern Pacific at Colorado City, to the south. Lumber and other supplies had to be hauled in by wagon from Colorado City, a major reason why most Scurry County pioneers lived in dugouts.

Like Billy Johnson, R. T. and Sallie Mellard made their home in a dugout on Block 2 of the H&TC grant. Mellard continued to head cattle drives, but in 1883 he erected a rock house with shed rooms. Also settling on Block 2 was another Johnson brother-in-law, A. E. Cressup, whose wife Mary was another of Billy's stepsisters.[14]

The Burnet County delegation made a significant contribution to early Scurry County. The census-taker for 1880 rode around the sparsely settled county—which had been created but not yet organized—and could find only 102 citizens. But as the parade from Burnet County suggests, growth was steady. Organized in 1876, Scurry County was one of thirteen frontier counties attached to Shackelford County for administrative purposes. To conduct official business, Scurry County residents had to ride to Albany, seat of Shackelford County. The State of Texas permitted a county to organize when at least 150 voters were in residence. In 1884 a petition to organize was submitted by Scurry County citizens. An election was duly held, Snyder became the county seat, and the first meeting of the Scurry County Commissioners Court convened on July 23, 1884.[15]

Progress of the new county was catalogued in 1887. That year a statewide statistical census was compiled, separate from any federal census. The *First Annual Report of the Agricultural Bureau* revealed that within seven years the population of Scurry County had grown to 434: "Males 244, females 190." There were seventy-eight families, with "a total school population of 134." The county seat, Snyder, claimed 300 residents, nearly three-quarters of the county's population. The only schoolhouse was a two-room structure in Snyder. There were four merchants, five lawyers, and one physician.

Only 616 acres were under cultivation in Scurry County. "Farming, as an independent pursuit, has not been followed to any considerable extent," concluded the report. "Stock raising is the principal industry of the people." There were 24,281 cattle in the county valued at $194,703. There also were 1,244 horses and mules, along with 21,496 sheep. Pasturage was plentiful, and there was no trouble between the cattlemen and sheepherders of Scurry County. [16]

During 1887 six couples were married in the county, but there were no divorces. Two citizens died, and there were four births—including Billy Johnson's second son.

As the young rancher industriously built up his holdings, he became the subject of matchmaking. Ophelia Sims Faught, Mollie Sims Wolf, and Billy Sims had a teenaged sister still living at the Burnet County home place. Nannie May Sims was born in 1865, and she was nineteen when Billy Johnson rode back to Burnet County to make her his bride.

Billy and Nannie were married on Tuesday, July 22, 1884. The couple posed for a wedding photo in a photography studio. The twenty-one-year-old groom sat in a low, overstuffed Victorian chair. He wore a light-colored suit with a wing-tipped collar and tie—and high-heeled cowboy boots. Nannie stood beside him in an elaborate wedding dress with fancy detail. From atop her head flowed a white, cathedral-length veil. The basic color of her dress was a light shade, accentuated with black cuffs, a large black bow, and black ruching at her breast. There was a scooped neck, topped by a lace insertion with black ribbon. The bodice was fitted, while the heavy taffeta skirt featured a draped tier.

The newlyweds journeyed to their ranch and dugout home. Billy added a room aboveground, creating a two-room, two-story residence.

Nannie Sims Johnson, who married a pioneer rancher and became the mother of the affable Emmett, the short-lived Joe, and the volatile Sid and Gladys. Courtesy Betty M. Giddens.

The children of Billy and Nannie Johnson, ca.
1900. Seated, Emmett (born 1885). Standing,
L to R: Sidney (born 1889), Joe (born 1887,
died in 1902 of blood poisoning), Gladys
(born 1891). Courtesy Scurry County Museum,
Snyder, Texas.

Pretty Nannie Johnson was not intimidated by the primitive nature of life on the West Texas frontier. She had sisters and a brother nearby, and during her girlhood Burnet County still had been subject to Comanche raids. Nannie was strong-minded and shared her husband's ambitions. She was regarded as "a fine cook," and while Billy Johnson kept a hired cook for his growing family, Nannie "carefully trained each person who worked in her kitchen."[17]

Billy and Nannie welcomed their first son, William Emmett, in September 1885. Two years later, in October 1887, Nannie gave her maiden name to Joe Sims Johnson. A third son, Sidney A., was born in October 1889. In February 1891 a daughter, Ida Gladys, completed the family unit. Billy hauled in lumber, shingles, and other materials for a two-story, L-shaped house. There was a well in the yard, and a spectacular view to the north from the mesa home site.

Billy taught all of his children, including Gladys, to ride and shoot. Although sidesaddles were in vogue for females, Billy regarded this style of riding as unsafe. Billy mounted his daughter atop a western stock saddle, directing Gladys to wear divided skirts of heavy serge and to ignore any comments about unladylike attire. All four children were expected to help with ranch work. Billy liked to spoil his little girl, but Nannie disapproved, and clashed with Gladys.

School terms in Texas during the late nineteenth century added up to no more than seven months for the year. The Ennis Creek School, a one-room rural school was built a couple of miles west of the Johnson Ranch. But Emmett, Joe, Sid, and Gladys received most of their schooling in Snyder, where a spacious two-room frame building was erected in 1885. The Snyder Public Free School District offered ten grades. Pupils entered the first grade at age eight, a common practice throughout Texas, where many rural children had to walk a couple of miles or more through unsettled countryside. Nannie took her children to Snyder to live during school terms, returning to the ranch on weekends.[18]

When Billy Johnson drove his family to town, he hitched up Dock and Dandy, a matched pair of bay trotters. Billy liked to time his fine

Billy Johnson's ranch house north of Snyder in 1910. The family stands on the porch. L to R: Gladys, Sid, Emmett, Joe, Billy, and Nannie. Note the well in the yard. Courtesy Scurry County Museum, Snyder, Texas.

South side of the Snyder square in 1887. Courtesy Scurry County Museum, Snyder, Texas.

team from gate to gate, and the trips to Snyder often were made at a spirited pace. Church services were held irregularly in the Ennis Creek School, but as in other aspects of their life, the Johnsons harbored higher aspirations for church. In 1883 Billy and Nannie Johnson helped found Snyder's First Methodist Church.[19]

While Billy and Nannie were raising their children, he continued to expand the Johnson Ranch, despite drought during the 1880s. Billy acquired forty-seven deeded sections, and he leased other parcels.[20] A section of land is one mile long and one mile wide, encompassing 640 acres. Billy Johnson therefore owned 30,080 acres of rangeland, watered by Ennis Creek and lesser streams. Ennis Creek is spring-fed and has never run dry. A common method of land acquisition by big ranchers like Billy Johnson was for cowboys on the ranch payroll to file on a section adjacent to the home ranch, and then deed it over to the rancher.

Farmers began to try their luck in Scurry County, sometimes nesting on rangeland they did not own, then putting up barbed wire fences to protect their cultivated fields from grazing cattle. Some of these squatters tried to settle on land owned or leased by Billy Johnson. He ejected them, by persuasion if possible, or by force if necessary. One of his riders during this period was Tom Farley, known for his skill with guns.[21]

But travelers always were welcome at the Johnson Ranch, parking their wagons in front of the house and eating with the family in the dining room, before retiring outside to their bedrolls. Visitors sometimes were able to enjoy horse-breaking activities on the flat in front of the house. Billy Johnson did not raise many horses, preferring to purchase riding stock as needed. These young horses had to be "rough broke" before being put to work, so from time to time informal rodeos provided exciting entertainment for the ranch community. In 1900 Johnson's mount unexpectedly threw his head back. Struck in the mouth, Johnson lost three teeth, necessitating a trip to Colorado for dental repairs.[22]

When he was twenty-six, in 1888, Billy Johnson was elected a county commissioner from Precinct Two, the northeast quarter of Scurry County. Johnson was re-elected in 1890, but thereafter he stayed out of politics and concentrated on business. As he accumulated working capital, Billy Johnson gravitated into banking. Johnson and another successful early rancher, George Smith, were among the founders of the First National Bank of Snyder. Smith served as bank president, but when he died in 1902 Johnson assumed the presidency.[23]

Through his bank and in other ways Johnson helped new settlers get a start in Scurry County. In 1897 newlyweds Perry and Dora Morris moved into a dugout on Ennis Creek. Perry was hired as a ranch hand by Billy Johnson, who provided badly needed wages as the young couple began developing their new claim. Also in 1897 Fielder Helms brought his wife and three children to a four-section claim in northeast Scurry County. (The previous year, the State Legislature passed the Four-Section Act, selling 2,560-acre claims to settlers in West Texas.) After spending two years with his family in a dugout, Helms traded two steers to Billy Johnson for a two-room frame house with a sleeping loft. The house had been built by aspiring rancher Rich Miller on land later acquired by Johnson. Helms hauled the house to his claim and later added a wing.[24]

Since entering Scurry County as a sixteen-year-old drover, Billy Johnson had built an impressive ranching operation, become a loving husband and father, won election to public office, and become a bank president. Although he was a tough-minded cattle baron and pragmatic businessman, Johnson was generous to his friends and neighbors, who affectionately called him "Uncle Billy." By the time he reached forty, Johnson enjoyed prosperity and success in all aspects of life. In a new century he had every reason to expect even greater prosperity and continued success and happiness.

The Sims Family

Samuel David "Dave" Sims (1857–1919)
Laura Belle Smith Sims (1865–1956)

    Ada Pearl (1882–1956)
    Edward Caldwell (1884–1916)
    Sallie Ethel (1886–1983)
    U. B. "Kelly" (1888–1957)
    Samuel David Jr. (1890–1962)
    Eva (1892–1979)
    Lee Roy (1895–1969)
    John Tom "Red" (1899–1975)
    Golda Belle (1901–1987)
    Georgia Leon (1904–1964)

Chapter 3

Dave Sims, Cattle Baron

"The changeable weather, the distances, the soil, and the loneliness were merely hardships or dangers to be overcome."

T. R. Fehrenbach, Texas historian

While Billy Johnson was progressing from teenage cowboy to pioneer rancher to family man to cattle baron, Dave Sims was following a similar trail. Five years older than Billy Johnson, Dave was born during a family migration from Arkansas to Lampasas County in the Hill Country of Texas. On July 6, 1857, Samuel David Sims was born in a covered wagon in Rusk County, amid the Piney Woods of East Texas. His father was David Sims, and his mother was Frances Emeline Sparks Sims. At twenty-six Emeline was the mother of three daughters and, now, a baby boy. Her parents were Samuel and Sarah Sparks, and she named her son after her father and her husband.[1]

Samuel Sparks was a farmer, born in Maryland, raised in Georgia, and married in Alabama. Acquiring a few slaves to provide labor, Samuel restlessly moved from one frontier farm to another. Emeline was born in Alabama in 1830, while her nine younger siblings were born in Mississippi and Arkansas. At nineteen Emeline married David Sims. Living near her patriarchal father, Emeline and David had three daughters in Arkansas: Malissa, Eliza, and Zebell.

Samuel and Sarah Sparks lost their two youngest children, but their three oldest daughters married and they began to enjoy grandchildren, while their four sons provided invaluable help on the farm. Samuel, however, could not resist the lure of new land in Texas, the nation's fastest-growing state during the 1850s. Although now in his fifties, the old pioneer farmer wanted one more fresh start. In 1857 Samuel Sparks led his extended family, along with livestock and household goods, to Lampasas County—a trek enlivened by the birth of Samuel David Sparks along the way.

Another pioneer rancher, John Higgins, also moved his family into Lampasas County in 1857. (His oldest son, six-year-old Pink, eventually would develop close connections with Billy Johnson in West Texas.) During the late 1850s there were Comanche raids throughout Lampasas County and vicinity, with horses stolen, cabins burned, children kidnapped, and settlers tortured, killed, and scalped. After two years of exposing himself, his wife and five children to mortal danger, Higgins pulled his family back two counties to the east, although they would return to Lampasas County in 1862.

Samuel Sparks, who had a squad of sons old enough to protect his home, did not move. The Sparks family purchased land on Sulphur Creek about three and one-half miles east of Lampasas. A pathway through the deep creek became known as Sparks Crossing. David Sims died not long after the migration to Lampasas County, and Emeline moved with her children into Lampasas. Nothing is known of David's fate, but he was not listed in the Census of 1860 for Lampasas County, while the occupation of twenty-nine-year-old Emeline was stated as "Household Affairs." Her oldest daughter, Malissa, was ten; Eliza was eight; Zebell, called "Bell," was seven; Dave was three.[2]

Despite the loss of his father, little David had a strong masculine presence in his life. His grandfather, Samuel Sparks, was vigorous and commanding in middle age. Samuel's four sons—Martin Van Buren, Samuel Jr., Thomas, and John—ranged in age from twenty-three to sixteen, just right to serve as role models, mentors, and objects of hero worship to their young nephew. The oldest Sparks son was born on March 4, 1837, the day Martin Van Buren was inaugurated as president. Named Martin Van Buren Sparks, he was called Van. Van Sparks read avidly, and he taught school in Arkansas and, in 1859, in Lampasas. Enlisting as a Confederate private in 1862, he quickly won promotion to sergeant major and served until the end of the war. After returning home he entered public affairs. Van was a justice of the peace, district clerk of Lampasas County for a decade, and presiding justice (today's county judge). Judge Sparks, as he was commonly called, was a deacon and church clerk of the First Baptist Church of Lampasas, and his son, Samuel, became a Baptist minister.[3]

In 1859 Van's brother, Samuel Jr., served in the Lampasas Guards, a militia unit organized to protect the county from Comanche marauders, and Sam also was a justice of the peace and county clerk. Thomas Sparks was a Confederate infantry sergeant, and later became an Idaho rancher and a member of the territorial legislature. The youngest brother, John, rode with a Home Guard company during the Civil War. By the late 1860s he was leading long drives throughout the cattle frontier. John put together a string of ranches in southern Idaho and northeastern Nevada, encompassing 300,000 acres and 40,000 head of cattle. John Sparks was elected governor of Nevada in 1902.[4]

Dave Sims was raised among males who were ambitious, responsible, and upwardly mobile. During his boyhood in the 1860s, Lampasas County was open range ranching country, and as Dave grew up he learned to ride, shoot, and handle livestock. But he also learned that men took responsibility for protecting and providing for their families. He absorbed the need to own and develop his own property, as well as the restless inclination to head west to re-establish himself. The ambitions and courage of pioneers ran strong in the blood of his family, and were passed on in full measure to little Dave Sims.

Dave lost his grandfather in 1871, when he was fourteen. Sixty-eight-year-old Samuel Sparks was accidentally killed while attempting to blast a water well through rocky soil on his land. He was buried near his home at Sparks Cemetery. Samuel was interred beside his third daughter, Elizabeth Sparks Denson. Elizabeth had married Shade Denson in Arkansas, and they were the first members of the Sparks tribe to move to Texas, three years before Samuel brought the rest of the family from Arkansas. Elizabeth died in 1861 at twenty-six, shortly after giving birth to her third child. [5]

Shade Denson became a Confederate captain during the Civil War, remarried, and had eight more children. He served as sheriff of Lampasas County from 1870 through 1874, and during a saloon fight in 1873, Sheriff Denson was severely wounded by Mark Short. Tom Sparks, Denson's former brother-in-law, tried to form a pursuit posse, but this effort was thwarted by several of the Horrell brothers, notorious as rustlers and gunmen. Three years later Short was arrested in another county and brought to Lampasas for trial. Denson's oldest son, Samuel W.—namesake of his grandfather and first cousin of Dave Sims—sought out Short in a saloon.

"Mark Short," announced Samuel, "you are my meat." He killed his father's attacker with three shots, and then escaped on horseback. Samuel rode to Montana and changed his name, but he would return to Lampasas in 1892 and win a not guilty verdict from a friendly jury.[6]

Saloon shootings were common in Lampasas during the 1870s. An especially wild gun battle erupted in 1873 in the Matador Saloon on the square. The Horrell brothers and several supporters gunned down a captain and three members of the State Police who had ridden from Austin to arrest them. Mart Horrell was seriously wounded and placed in custody, but his brothers engineered an escape. The entire clan left for lawless Lincoln County, New Mexico, where they triggered the bloody "Horrell War." After returning to Lampasas County, the surviving Horrell boys turned their thieving proclivities toward the cattle of Pink Higgins.

Higgins was a dangerous target. As a teenager he rode with pursuit posses after war parties or rustlers. Pink was wounded twice before Comanche raids finally subsided in the mid-1870s. He joined the Law and Order League, which spread across Texas during the turbulent years after the Civil War. When he was eighteen, Pink adjusted the noose around the neck of a rustler apprehended by a Law and Order League posse, which imposed summary execution across a branch of a hackberry tree.[7]

During the 1870s Pink formed his own ranch in Lampasas County and became active as a trail boss. When the Horrell brothers began stealing Pink's livestock, a blood feud exploded. Before Texas Rangers stopped the shooting in 1877, Pink killed Merritt Horrell in a Lampasas saloon and there was a major shootout on the town square, along with several smaller skirmishes. Pink was suspected of a major role in the deadly vendetta which followed, and of participating in the lynching of Mart and Tom Horrell.

Dave Sims turned twenty during the Horrell-Higgins Feud, but he was not involved in any of the violence that wracked Lampasas County. Like his uncles he worked on the family ranch, accumulating livestock of his own in the customary manner of wage payment. While there is no evidence that Dave participated in trail drives, so many herds were driven north from Lampasas County during the 1870s, it is likely that at least once he was among the nameless drovers who took part in the great adventure of the time.

When Dave was twenty-four he took part in an even more universal adventure. On January 7, 1882, Dave married Laura Belle Smith at her home in Burnet County. Her father was James Gibson Smith Jr., but he was called "Dandy Jim." Dandy Jim was from Tennessee, and he came to Texas with his brother Watt in 1848. For two years Dandy Jim and Watt worked on a ranch in Gonzales County. Then they rounded up and branded a herd of 300 brood mares and stallions, driving them to the open range country of northeastern Burnet County, which would not be organized until 1854. Jim built a log cabin on the banks of Rough Creek and utilized free grazing for his herd.

A few miles to the north, a settler named Christian James lived with his family beside the Lampasas River. Dandy Jim was smitten with one of the James daughters, Sarah, who was "the prettiest little filly I ever saw." Although Sarah was more than a decade younger than her suitor, she agreed to wed him. Dandy Jim and Sarah were married in 1854 and moved into his log cabin. He began to acquire title to acreage in 1857, in time accumulating nearly 6,000 acres. The first of eight children was born in 1857; there would be seven boys and one girl. Five of the boys—Jack, George, Lon, Dolph, and Oz—later moved to the Snyder area as ranchers and as bank partners with Billy Johnson.[8]

Laura Belle, the only daughter and fourth child, was born on January 17, 1865. Although her father added to the log cabin, it soon became too small for the growing Smith family. When Laura Belle was seven, in 1872, Dandy Jim built a spacious two-story frame home, with three doors, upstairs as well as downstairs, opening onto long front galleries. By 1881 Dave Sims was a visitor at this fine house. The Smith ranch was only about ten miles southeast of the Sparks ranch, not much of a ride for a young cowboy on a courting campaign.

Dave "dropped his rope on her" on January 7, 1882, ten days before Laura Belle turned seventeen. The wedding was conducted by Rev. L. R. Millican, pastor of the Burnet Baptist Church and soon to become famous as "The Cowboy Preacher." As a young cowboy Millican enjoyed watching fights in Lampasas saloons, but when he was twenty-two, in 1874, he found religion at a camp meeting. After becoming a preacher, Reverend Millican angrily retrieved a stolen horse from the Horrells, and while conducting graveside services for Merritt Horrell he warned the surviving brothers to look to their souls. During a long and fruitful ministry in West Texas, the Cowboy Preacher was instrumental in organizing the popular Paisano Baptist Encampment near Alpine, while pastoring—and often founding—Baptist churches in San Angelo, Midland, Pecos, Big Spring, El Paso, Fort Davis, Toyah, Van Horn, Odessa, Sierra Blanca, Clint, Fort Hancock, Presidio, and other communities. The Sims-Smith nuptials were officiated by a remarkable Baptist missionary.[9]

Dave and Laura Belle set up housekeeping about thirty miles northwest of Lampasas. Dave's connection with this location was his aunt, Eliza Sparks Bull. At the age of eighteen in 1851, Eliza had married Ambrose Bull in Arkansas. Bull was a widower, and Eliza became stepmother to his daughter, Susan Louisa—who later married Eliza's brother, Martin Van Buren Sparks. After the family migration to Texas, Ambrose and Eliza and their children settled northwest of Lampasas, in open range country that later became Mills County. The stream that watered their ranch was called Bull Creek.[10]

It is likely that Dave cowboyed for Ambrose Bull before his marriage. When Dave and his bride moved to the Bull Creek area, he almost certainly worked on shares for Ambrose, because he began accumulating a cattle herd. The Dave Sims brand was OXO.

Ten months after they married, on November 7, 1882, Dave and Laura Belle welcomed their first baby, Ada Pearl. Almost two years later their first son, Edward Caldwell, was born on July 26, 1884. Another daughter, Sallie Ethel, was born on November 18, 1886.[11]

While Dave and Laura Belle were bringing their first three children into the world, the country around them was settling up. In 1885 the Gulf, Colorado and Santa Fe Railroad laid track northwest from Lampasas, providing a connection with Galveston. Railroad official Joe Goldthwaite directed the sale of town lots at a site a few miles northeast of the Bull-Sparks cattle operation. The town of Goldthwaite began to grow beside the railroad tracks and in 1887 was named the seat of a new county. Mills County was organized from four surrounding counties: Lampasas, Brown, Hamilton, and Comanche.[12]

The influx of population stimulated by the new railroad caused a sudden rise in land values. By 1887 improved land in newly formed Mills County sold for five to fifteen dollars per acre, while unimproved land sold for one to five dollars.[13] Pioneer blood ran strong in the veins of Dave Sims, and by 1887 he was irresistibly pulled to move his ranch to new land. Although pregnant with their fourth child, Laura Belle— also from pioneer stock—strongly supported the move. Packing their belongings into covered wagons and rounding up their livestock, the Sims family headed northwest to found a frontier ranch.

Several years earlier, three of Laura Belle's brothers—George, Jack, and Lon Smith—had driven a cattle herd from Burnet County to Kent County, which was not yet organized. Soon the brothers went their separate ways within the region but Laura Belle liked the description of the open rangelands in Kent County. Sight unseen, she put money down through "an Austin lawyer" on Kent County land.[14]

But Dave Sims was determined to start a ranch in New Mexico, and the OXO herd was driven across West Texas. At the New Mexico border, however, cattle inspectors detected hoof and mouth disease. Dave was prohibited from bringing his livestock into New Mexico, and the Sims party turned back toward West Texas. En route to the land Laura Belle had purchased, she gave birth to her fourth child. Uvalde Burns Sims—always called "Kelly"—was born on February 6, 1888. Like his father, Kelly Sims was birthed in a covered wagon while his family moved to a new ranch home.

The Sims property included a creek that flowed freely and had a swimming hole. A dugout was fashioned near Sims Creek and in 1890 the census-taker included directions to this crude family dwelling.

The 1890 census recorded only 324 residents on forty-eight ranches and farms. Dave and Laura Belle added to this scant population with their fifth child. Samuel David Sims Jr., was born in the dugout on March 18, 1890.

While Dave Sims expanded his property, OXO cattle grazed free on unclaimed range. But in rugged, mostly treeless, sparsely settled Kent County, land was available and cheap. Sims rapidly acquired parcel after parcel, finally owning title to forty sections. There was less rainfall than in Lampasas County, which averaged twenty-nine inches per year, to less than twenty-three in Kent County. Sims decided to run twenty-five cows and a bull per section, which meant the OXO herd would aggregate well over one thousand head, plus calves. He also worked at breeding good cow ponies, and in time demand developed for mares from the Sims ranch.[15]

Sims had to move his growing family to more spacious quarters than a dugout. The nearest railroad point was Colorado City, more than fifty miles to the south, and Dave hauled in wagonloads of lumber and shingles to his isolated ranch. The building site was more than two miles from the dugout, near the swimming hole on Sims Creek.

The long front porch of the Sims ranch house faces east and was screened in for sleeping. Photo by the author.

The north wing of the main house contained the kitchen, in the rear, and an upstairs bedroom where the boys slept. Photo by the author.

The ranch house was big but plain, with none of the Victorian architectural flourishes which adorned many residences of the 1890s. In style and floor plan, the Sims house was a throwback to homes of an earlier Texas frontier. Two large front rooms were bisected by an enclosed dogtrot (it had become customary by the 1890s to enclose open dogtrots, thereby creating a central hallway). Each of the front rooms boasted a fireplace. A long gallery, or porch, extended across the entire front of the house, and later would be screened in. Stacked behind the front room on the right of the hallway were three more rooms. The back room of this L-wing was the kitchen. Above the back two rooms was a large bedroom where the boys slept. There were no inner walls or insulation and during northers and winter cold spells the interior was frigid, except directly in front of the fireplaces.[16]

A board and batten smokehouse was erected a few steps back of the kitchen porch. A short distance south of the ranch house a smaller residence was built. This house was erected for Dave's spinster sisters, Eliza and Bell. Only a year and a half apart in age, Eliza and Bell never married and were extremely close. While Dave made a new home for his family in West Texas, Eliza and Bell lived in Belton. Eliza turned forty in 1891, and Bell in March 1893. They journeyed to remote Kent County and moved into the smaller house on the Sims ranch. There were no close neighbors, no towns, no schools, and no churches. The family had a Baptist tradition, but there was no church closer than Snyder in the next county. Eliza and Bell brought their nieces and nephews into their home to teach the three Rs.

Once a year Dave drove a wagon into Snyder for flour, coffee, salt, sugar, and other provisions that could not be produced on the ranch. One year, while returning to the ranch with a heavily loaded wagon, Dave met an emigrant wagon. The driver told Dave that his wife and children were starving, and he pleaded for food. While Dave put together a supply sack, the father proffered a fiddle in a case. Too proud to accept outright charity, the father insisted on a "trade." Dave accepted the fiddle, and the musical instrument and its case today is a family heirloom.[17]

The board-and-batten smokehouse was built just behind the main house, handy to the kitchen. Photo by the author.

A short distance south of the main ranch house, Dave Sims erected a smaller frame dwelling for his spinster sisters, Belle and Eliza. In their home, ranch children were taught the three Rs. Photo by the author.

Homemade rocking chairs with cowhide seats used by Dave and Laura Belle Sims. Today these heirlooms are preserved by Ed and Anne Sims. Photo by the author.

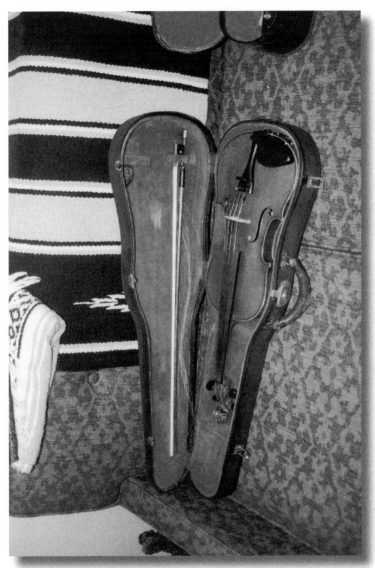

Fiddle traded by a starving family for food to Dave Sims. Ed and Anne have preserved the fiddle. Photo by the author.

In 1892 Kent County was organized. Clairemont, established near the center of the county in 1888 by a rancher whose daughter was named Claire, became the county seat. Lumber was hauled all the way from Colorado City as Clairemont began to take shape. Red sandstone was quarried east of town for a two-story courthouse and a jail. By 1900 there were stores, a post office, a bank, a newspaper, and a hotel. Clairemont had a 1900 population of sixty-five, while the county totaled 899 residents, 134 farms and ranches, and more than 29,000 head of cattle. [18]

Clairemont was about thirteen miles from the Sims ranch along primitive roads. Although Snyder was farther away, it was a considerably larger town than Clairemont. The tiny community of Polar began to grow up about nine miles west of the ranch. A rural school eventually was formed, along with a church, but Polar was never more than a hamlet. The Sims family made their home in a lonely region of rugged beauty.

Sims children continued to be born at regular intervals. Eva appeared in 1892, and Lee Roy joined the family in 1895. John Tom, called "Red" or "Booger," was born in 1899, while Golda Belle came along two years later. The tenth and final child, Georgia, was born on December 1, 1904, when Laura Belle was thirty-nine. [19]

Large families were common in America during the eighteenth and nineteenth centuries. In modern society children are expensive to raise and families usually are small. But during earlier centuries, when a majority of Americans were farmers or stock raisers, children were an economic asset. Strapping sons provided greatly needed labor on a farm or ranch, while girls offered invaluable help with time-consuming women's tasks.

Dave and Laura Belle produced five sons between 1884 and 1899: Ed, Kelly, Dave, Lee Roy, and Red. The girls could ride and help with ranch work. But with five sons scattered over a fifteen-year span, Dave and Laura Belle were assured of a continuous stream of family cowboys on the ranch. The large Sims family provided their own company in a sparsely settled country. Laura Belle, Eliza, and Bell gave

Kelly Sims, like his father, was born in a covered wagon, during his family's trek to West Texas. Raised a cowboy, Kelly became a lifelong rancher. Courtesy Ed Sims.

Dave Sims (right) sitting on the steps of his ranch house with his son Kelly. Courtesy Ed Sims.

each other the feminine companionship of a trio of adult women. At any given time there were children of every age around the big ranch house, and they grew up as playmates. Domestic chores were handled by the adult women and the older daughters. The older boys rode with their father, who also directed the work of cowboy employees. The OXO cattle were scattered across a range that stretched for miles. Although there was little timber, the terrain was rocky and broken, and roundup work challenged riders and their horses.

T. R. Fehrenbach observed that "this was a tremendously exhilarating time for a strong man." Dave Sims was a strong man, and the daily experience of riding his own range—even if it was isolated—was deeply exhilarating. "The Texan, like all Westerners, was not antisocial, but asocial," stated Fehrenbach. "No other breed, probably, could have lived contently for years on a far-flung frontier, where the distances between houses or farms were measured in miles." Dave Sims was of this breed, and he embodied Fehrenbach's description. "Big country, even terrible country as Texas could be in the western counties, fed big dreams . . . . The changeable weather, the distances, the soil, and the loneliness were merely hardships or dangers to be overcome."[20]

Dave Sims and his family overcame hardships and loneliness together. They were self-reliant on their isolated ranch, and like many frontier families they became close-knit, with unwavering loyalty to one another. By the time that Georgia, the last child, was born in December 1904, the oldest siblings were old enough to marry and establish their own homes. Indeed, both Ada, twenty-two, and Ed, twenty, were courting and would marry within months. But the family ties forged on the home ranch would prove unbreakable, even in the face of mortal tragedy.

Laura Belle Sims, mother of ten and matriarch of a West Texas ranching family. Courtesy Ed Sims.

Chapter 4

Gladys and Ed

"A pair of star-cross'd lovers . . . ."

Romeo and Juliet

Gladys was the princess of the Johnson ranch. She was the baby of the family and the only daughter. And she was the apple of her father's eye. After three sons, Billy Johnson was ready for a daddy's little girl. He spoiled his daughter and let her have her way and shielded her from the anger of her mother. And ultimately she drove him to despair.

Emmett Johnson was five-and-a-half-years-old when his baby sister was born. The oldest Johnson son was affable and even-tempered, kind and generous—as a boy and as a man. Joe was three-and-a-half when Gladys was born, and like Emmett he was a genial big brother. But Sid was only sixteen months older than Gladys. Close in age, they also shared such traits as willfulness, nerve, hot tempers, and ruthless determination to have their own way. They grew up as playmates, companions, confidants, and accomplices—in matters small and large.

Billy Johnson taught all of his children to ride. Although full-skirted female attire of the 1890s demanded sidesaddles for equestriennes, Billy—a lifelong horseman—knew that stride riding was safer. Perhaps, too, the little girl wanted to ride like her brothers, and many western women shunned sidesaddles while riding.

"Her father ordered her to wear a divided skirt of heavy serge and not to be bothered by what people would say . . .," related Lois Lucie Curnette, a family friend. "Her first ride in this get-up was to Camp Springs where her father was to receive some cattle. A picnic was being held at Dripping Springs that day, and soon everyone in that end of the county was aware of her unladylike attire."[1]

Gladys loved to ride, sometimes with her father or brothers, sometimes alone. Like her brothers, she was taught to shoot, and she always carried a gun. Gladys and her mother frequently squabbled. Perhaps, like many other mothers and daughters, they were too much alike to enjoy a harmonious relationship, or perhaps an annoyed Nannie tried to exert discipline over a spoiled daughter. When the exchange between Billy's wife and little girl became too heated, he would tactfully intercede.

"Let's go riding in the pasture," Billy would suggest, and daddy and daughter would set off on a cross-country ride. Both strong-minded Johnson females had time to cool off, but Nannie doubtless would have appreciated more support from her husband.[2]

Gladys's solitary rides across the big Johnson range may have been noticed by a couple of men, or her encounter with two men while riding may have been accidental. But according to family legend, while Gladys was alone on horseback she was accosted by two men. Without hesitation the girl produced her pistol and killed both men or wounded both men or drove them off. Gladys's youngest daughter, Beverly, told the author that both men were shot, and that the incident was "covered up" by Billy Johnson.

Wealthy and influential, Billy Johnson certainly was capable of covering up a violent incident for his daughter, as he would prove several years later. Such a cover-up would require legal help, and Johnson retained skillful lawyers to keep his land titles clear and tend to other legal matters.

If Gladys, in early adolescence, successfully defended herself with a handgun against assailants, then was protected by her father with a cover-up, she would have absorbed a critical and formative lesson. In future crises Gladys was quick to bring her gun into play, confident that her father would provide a legal safety net from the most serious of incidents.

When Gladys was eleven, in 1902, her brother Joe died of blood poisoning. This fatal affliction was not uncommon on a ranch with rusty barbed wire everywhere. Joe was only fifteen, and his premature loss was merely the first of the tragedies that would bring torment to the Johnson family.

As a girl Gladys rode with Sid, and perhaps her other brothers, to the nearby Ennis Creek School. Then she attended school in Snyder with her brothers. During school terms Nannie and her children lived in town on weekdays, returning to the ranch on weekends and holidays. Like all youngsters raised on a ranch but sent to town for school, the Johnson kids always were elated to get back to their home and horses.

In the fall of 1905, when Emmett had just turned twenty and Sid was almost sixteen, the two surviving Johnson sons were sent to the New Mexico Military Institute at Roswell, nearly 250 miles to the west. It seems likely that this educational effort may have been aimed at Sid, who was high-strung and probably needed discipline as much as academic instruction.

The Johnson boys enrolled on September 27 in the high school department. The Institute included a college, but completion of high school required eleven grades, and the Snyder schools had only ten. Emmett was classified a senior, even though he was older than many of the college students, while Sidney was placed in the junior class. Students wore uniforms—khaki trousers, blue tunics, blue military caps—but Sid failed to adjust to the regimen or to the more rigorous level of academics. After six weeks, on November 9, Sid withdrew from school and returned to his father's ranch. Emmett, mature and congenial, applied himself throughout the school year. He posed with his fellow seniors—the college "Class of '10"—for a class photograph and graduated in May 1906. But Emmett had no intention of beginning a four-year college program at the age of twenty-one, and he resumed life as a West Texas rancher.[3]

Gladys was taken off to the renowned North Texas Female College and Conservatory of Music in Sherman, fifty miles north of Dallas. Supported by the Methodist denomination, this school had been guided since 1888 by a legendary female educator, Mrs. Lucy Kidd, a widow. (Later Mrs. Kidd was remarried, to Methodist bishop Joseph Key, and the school became known as Kidd-Key College.) Mrs. Kidd appointed noted European music teachers and the college acquired 120 pianos, while annual enrollment exceeded 500.

Gladys, accompanied almost certainly by one or both parents, enrolled as a freshman on Tuesday, October 25, 1904, a year before Emmett and Sid were packed off to New Mexico. The fall semester started several weeks before Gladys arrived, so a discount was provided on tuition ($16.25 instead of $25.00) and on room and board ($61.75 instead of $95.00). This late enrollment might be explained by the obscure shooting incident involving Gladys. She was only thirteen in the fall of 1904, but if she had used her gun against assailants in, say, early October, it may have seemed prudent to whisk her away from Scurry County immediately. Or, since it is unknown when her romance with Ed Sims began, perhaps her parents made a sudden decision to send her off to college. Her age was not much of a factor, because many "colleges" of the period generally enrolled students of secondary age. The Johnsons had the means to place their daughter in a quality boarding school where she could acquire polish, and for whatever reason Gladys was brought to the North Texas College for Females late in October 1904.

Gladys Johnson became one of forty-four members of the freshman class of 1904. She was placed in standard lecture courses and in "Physical Culture" classes, but the curriculum emphasized music instruction. The charges to her account for music classes exceeded her basic tuition expenses, and she also was charged for sheet music and for practice sessions. Her new home was a shared bedroom in one of several dormitory cottages which stood beside the red brick classroom buildings. Mrs. Kidd enforced a strict dress code and mandatory church attendance, and she required chaperones for off-campus excursions into Sherman. Perhaps to acquire spending money for these trips, Gladys periodically charged modest amounts of "Cash"—usually seventy-five cents—to her account. In the yearbook photograph of the freshman class, Gladys appears demure and ladylike, and every bit as pretty as anyone in the group.[4]

Following her late start, the only break in her school year was the Christmas holiday. During the Christmas seasons of this era, Snyder's social scene was unusually lively. Frank Mellard, a young cowboy and future rancher—and a distant cousin of the Johnsons—reminisced that in Snyder "there would be parties somewhere almost every night—sometimes as many as eight or ten nights before and after Christmas. Some men would write a list of all of the young ladies' names, and a boy would select one and write her a note." Mellard, who was the son of rancher R. T. Mellard, added that "Snyder was just a Western cow town where everyone knew everyone else and the parties were a lot of fun."[5]

Gladys was petite and pretty, with her dark hair piled high in a pompadour, and certainly she was known by everyone. But after the party/holiday season, she returned by train to Sherman early in 1905 to finish the last two weeks of the fall term. Then the spring term began, on January 17, and Gladys attended classes through May and finished her freshman year. But when she returned to her home in June, Gladys had little intention of resuming her studies as a sophomore.

Throughout the spring semester Gladys bought a great many postage stamps, and it is tempting to surmise that she carried on a heavy correspondence with a sweetheart. At a holiday party or through some other connection Gladys had caught the eye of Ed Sims. It was no more than a dozen miles cross-country from the Sims ranch to the Johnson ranch—about the same distance that Dave Sims had to ride from his grandfather's ranch to Laura Belle's Burnet County home. Quite possibly Gladys and Ed had known each other for years. Their fathers were large-scale ranchers who at least occasionally must have had dealings with one another. Furthermore, in West Texas there were fellow immigrants from Burnet or

Lampasas counties who were mutual acquaintances—friends, neighbors, and relatives.

Ed was seven years older than Gladys. Even if they had been acquainted in earlier years, Gladys now had matured physically and had acquired poise in college. Ed was attracted by her fresh good looks—trim figure, blue eyes, pouty lips—as well as by her feisty personality. At twenty-one Ed was tall and broad-shouldered, with handsome features and neatly combed hair. It was time for him to make his own way in the world of ranching and, in addition to Gladys's other attractions, she was the daughter of a wealthy man. And Billy Johnson indeed would generously live up to expectations, providing a substantial dowry for his daughter when she married.

Ed stated in later years that he "dearly loved" Gladys.[6] Certainly love was in the air among the older siblings in the Sims household. Ada was in love with T. G. "Gee" McMeans, who had worn a badge in Ector County and as a Texas Ranger, and who bought and sold horses. On April 23, 1905, Ada became the first of the ten Sims children to marry. She was twenty-two and Gee was twenty-nine. Within a year the first Sims grandchild, Walter McMeans, was born.[7]

Just four months after Ada's wedding, Ed followed her to the altar. Gladys was only fourteen, but Ed's mother had been sixteen (soon to turn seventeen) when she married. Of course, fourteen was two crucial years younger than sixteen, even in a time and place when girls married young. Gladys's mother was twenty when she became Mrs. W. A. Johnson. Like any mother would be, Nannie Johnson was unhappy at the prospect of such an early marriage. No doubt she expressed herself pointedly, and she never relented in her antagonism against Ed. Billy Johnson surely would have agreed with the Capulet father of young Juliet: "Let two more summers wither in their pride / Ere we may think her ripe to be a bride."[8]

Ed and Gladys were undeterred by parental disapproval. Ed was in love and ready to take a bride. Gladys had, at the very least, a schoolgirl crush on her good-looking beau. And she felt ready to leave home. Perhaps she feared that her mother might again send her off for her sophomore year at college; perhaps Nannie had threatened to send Gladys away to separate her from Ed. Gladys was not the first girl to rush into marriage.

Ed and Gladys were married on Thursday, August 31, 1905.[9] In their wedding photograph Gladys, beautifully coiffed and dressed, appears older than her fourteen years—probably a reflection of the year spent at a quality boarding school. But she also looks stiff and irritated, as though the newlyweds have just quarreled, perhaps about how to stand or sit for their wedding portrait. Ed looks wide-eyed and a bit stunned, possibly having just experienced his bride's short fuse for the first time.

But Ed and Gladys made a fine-looking couple. Gladys later insisted that she was "a dutiful wife, and managed her household life with prudence and economy . . . ." Ed contended that for several years he and Gladys "lived together . . . as husband and wife in love and happy quietude . . . ."[10] In addition to happy quietude there was healthy passion. Less than two years after the marriage, on July 15, 1907, Gladys gave birth to a daughter, Helen Trix Sims. Usually called Trix, she was the first grandchild of the Johnson family, the second for the big Sims tribe. A couple of years later, on November 7, 1909, another daughter, Mildred Beverly, was welcomed by Gladys and Ed.

Billy Johnson provided a ranch in newly organized Garza County for Gladys and her family. Johnson invested $25,000 in land, cattle, fencing, corrals, and a new house with a big porch.[11] Ed brought to the operation livestock he had accumulated, horses as well as cattle, along with a section of land donated by his father from the Sims ranch. The new home of Gladys and Ed was thirty miles west of the Sims ranch and forty miles northwest of the Johnson ranch. Snyder was almost fifty miles distant.

But fourteen miles north of the ranch, Post City was taking shape. Founded in 1907, Post City was the creation of cereal magnate C. W. Post, who had determined to build a model community in West Texas. Born in Illinois in 1854, Post was a successful salesman and inventor of agricultural machinery. In 1886 business ventures brought him to Texas, where he lived on a ranch outside of Fort Worth. By the 1890s Post was suffering health problems from overwork. While ailing, he

The wedding portrait of Ed Sims, twenty-one, and Gladys Johnson, fourteen. Courtesy Charles Anderson, Sr.

responded to a recipe idea suggested by a ranch wife and developed a coffee substitute that he labeled Postum. He manufactured Postum at a plant at Battle Creek, Michigan. Soon he added the breakfast cereals Post Toasties and Grape Nuts. Post was an advertising genius, and by the early twentieth century he was a multimillionaire.[12]

Moved by the philanthropic impulses common to wealthy men of the Progressive Era, Post decided upon a West Texas colonization project that would offer families the opportunity to purchase homes or farms at low monthly payments. In 1906 he bought more than 213,000 acres of land along the Caprock, and began experimenting with irrigation and farming methods on land that formerly had grazed buffaloes and cattle.

Triggered by the promise of Post's activities and advertising, Garza County was organized in 1907. Post laid out a town site near the center of the new county, and Post City became the county seat. Post erected a big department store and scores of houses: one-, two-, three-, and four-bedroom residences, ranging from $800 to $6,000. One of his favorite construction projects was the thirty-room Algerita Hotel, which he provided with a chef, fine linens, and Post cereals on every breakfast table. He built, equipped, and staffed the two-story Post Sanitarium, the finest hospital in the region. Main Street was 120 feet wide, with grass, trees, and flowers enclosed boulevard style by a white picket fence. Post had high concrete curbs built, so that women could step easily from their carriages.

The town was surrounded by 160-acre farms, available from Post at generous terms. To provide adequate rainfall, Post tried seeding the clouds from firing stations along the nearby rim of the Caprock. In 1912 alone more than 24,000 pounds of dynamite were detonated in generally unproductive attempts to produce rain. Post hired a geologist to locate oil, and he constructed an enormous cotton mill which would provide hundreds of jobs. He also had a recreational lake built near town, and Two Draw Lake became a regional oasis and the site of an annual Fourth of July celebration.

A rare candid photograph from 1912 shows C. W. Post striking a characteristic pose in cowboy boots and Stetson hat. BHL

C. W. Post, with cigar, Stetson and lace-up boots, in West Texas in 1912. Courtesy Garza County Museum.

Two views of Post City in 1909, as the town rapidly took shape under the financial stimulus of C. W. Post. The long building is the Algerita Hotel, photographed from the roof or second floor of the new courthouse. Courtesy Garza County Museum.

Built in 1912, the Post Sanitarium was the first hospital in the region. State-of-the-art facilities included an X-ray lab, operating rooms, a specialized kitchen, and all private rooms with steam heat. Today the building houses the Garza County Museum. Photo by the author.

Post attracted a railroad which reached Post City late in 1910, permitting the regular arrival of building materials. Soon the population approached 1,000, and a school and churches were organized. Post installed a telephone exchange, while residents of Post City enjoyed running water. Across Main Street and half a block west of the Algerita Hotel stood the two-story stone courthouse. Both the Algerita and the Garza County courthouses would become sites of events crucial to the sad ending of the marriage of Ed and Gladys Sims.

During the same year that Post City was founded and that Ed and Gladys welcomed their first daughter, Emmett Johnson followed his little sister into matrimony. On Sunday afternoon, May 5, 1907, Emmett and Rocky Higgins were married at the Snyder home of Judge Cullen Higgins.[13] Rocky was the daughter of Pink Higgins, and Cullen was the firstborn of the old Lampasas County feudist.

Pink Higgins had followed his son and numerous other adventurous spirits from Lampasas County (and Burnet County) to this area of West Texas. Following the Horrell-Higgins Feud, Pink continued to headquarter at his Lampasas County ranch while remaining active as a trail driver. His frequent absences encouraged an affair between his wife, Betty, and a store clerk named Dunk Harris. When Pink learned of her unfaithfulness, he loaded Betty into a buggy and sent her packing with only her clothes and her daughter from a previous marriage (her first husband died young). Pink did not shoot Dunk Harris, perhaps because he wanted to avoid legal charges while he was responsible for three children.[14]

Cullen was five years old, Malinda was three, and Tom was one when Pink expelled their mother from the ranch. Pink's parents lived on the ranch and helped with the children, but when the divorce was finalized, on May 24, 1882, Pink was leading a trail drive toward Dodge City. Recognizing that his children needed a stepmother, Pink soon found a new wife in pretty Lena Rivers Sweet, daughter of a lawman killed in the line of duty. Pink and Lena married on June 8, 1883. He was thirty-two and she was fifteen. Lena brought a sweet and loving temperament to the marriage, and she earned the devotion of her stepchildren.

Pink and Lena had six children of their own, five girls and a boy. Their first child was born in 1886 and, utilizing Lena's middle name, the parents dubbed their baby Rocky Rivers Higgins. Their next little girl was named Ruby Lake Higgins, and their third daughter was christened Bonnie Bay Higgins. These nautical names ended with their only son, Roy, who was followed by Lorena ("Rena") and Nell. Pink had nine children, the most of any frontier shootist, and he was a devoted father.

He also remained a tall, intimidating man with a reputation as a killer. In 1891 a Lampasas County jury convicted him of cattle theft, involving a single "wild stag" (hair had grown over the brand) that he had received in a livestock trade brokered by an agent. That such flimsy charges resulted in a conviction clearly was a result of old grudges and a maturing community ready to rid itself of a forty-year-old relic of its rowdy frontier period. Pink was confined for nearly two years in the state's new penitentiary at Rusk in East Texas.[15]

John Higgins came to East Texas to be near his incarcerated son. While Pink's mother and second wife tended the children at the Lampasas County ranch at Higgins Mountain, John brought his adolescent grandsons to East Texas with a plan to further their educations. Fifteen-year-old Cullen attended Kilgore Business College, while twelve-year-old Tom enrolled in Tyler Commercial College. "College" was a loose term among educational institutions of the 1890s, often providing secondary instruction to youthful students. John Higgins may have stayed with his younger grandson in Tyler, which was a little more than forty miles northwest of Rusk.[16] Kilgore was about the same distance northeast of the prison town. Both Tyler and Kilgore were within a short railroad visit to Rusk Penitentiary.

When Pink returned to Lampasas County he found that a number of his old friends and allies had moved to West Texas. Bill Wren, for example, one of Pink's closest comrades, served two terms as sheriff of Lampasas County during the 1890s, but after leaving office he moved his family to Scurry County. In 1899 Pink lined up a job as range rider, or stock detective, for the vast Spur Ranch, which sprawled across more than half a million acres of rangeland in Kent, Garza, Crosby, and Dickens counties. The cattle herd exceeded 54,000 head and there were 800 horses. Livestock theft from the Spur Ranch was rampant.

Pink acquired a small parcel of land in northwestern Kent County and sent for his family. Lena soon arrived with their five daughters (Roy, an epileptic, had died in boyhood). Malinda, Pink's daughter by his first wife, was married and remained in Lampasas County. Tom Higgins chose to make his career in Lampasas, eventually serving sixteen years as county judge, but often visited his family in West Texas. Within a few years Pink's sister and brother-in-law, Malinda Jane and Tom Terry, left Lampasas County, settling with their eight children about four miles west of Roby in Fisher County.[17]

Pink's oldest son was part of the family migration to West Texas. Cullen Higgins grew into a fine and decent man, filled with ambition and energy. He read law in an attorney's office, acquired his license, and opened a practice in Fort Worth. But Fort Worth was a bustling city of 25,000, and Cullen soon decided to find a smaller town where there were fewer lawyers. In 1899 the twenty-three-year-old son of a pioneer moved to Snyder, confident that he could make a future for himself in the growing West Texas community.[18]

Cullen was an able and industrious lawyer, and after just three years in town, in 1902, he was elected to a four-year term as district attorney. In 1906, at the age of thirty, Cullen became the youngest district judge in Scurry County history, and he would respectfully be called "Judge" for the rest of his life. After leaving office four years later, Judge Higgins conducted a busy practice in all of the counties which he had served on the bench.[19]

"Now there was a great man," reminisced Lena Hopson Powell, who had known Cullen during her girlhood, when he was a close friend of her father. "He was one of the handsomest men I have ever seen in my life. He looked a lot like [actor] Robert Young . . . , same sparkling brown eyes, and same smile. And he had a million dollar personality."[20]

Popular and civic-minded, Higgins became a community leader and a stalwart of the First Methodist Church. "He was an open-minded Christian gentleman, a friend of every worthy interest, and was mindful at all times of the happiness and welfare of others," related the *Snyder Signal.* "He was a very busy lawyer, but always had time to render public service when needed."[21] Cullen married Olive Smith, who was a few years his senior, and they had a son, Marshall, in 1910.

Cullen's most important client was Billy Johnson, and the lawyer rented office space on the second floor of Johnson's First National Bank building. A fixture in Cullen's office suite was Rocky Higgins, who went to work for her older half-brother in her late teens. Bright and capable, she traveled with Cullen to various courthouses for days at a time, and she also worked as a court clerk. Rocky and Emmett Johnson encountered each other often enough to become sweethearts.

By 1906 Rocky and Emmett were in love. Rocky turned twenty in 1906, while Emmett was a year older. A good deal of their courtship had to be carried on through correspondence, because Rocky often was out of town on legal business with Cullen, while Emmett alternated building fence at a Johnson property in Kent County or running the home ranch while his parents were in Snyder ("I will be head boss while they are gone," wrote Emmett to his sweetheart. "Do you think I will be a good one?"). Little wonder that this peripatetic couple became engaged by correspondence.[22]

Throughout their correspondence Rocky tried to persuade Emmett to stop smoking cigarettes. She was elated in November 1906 when a letter from Emmett arrived with a packet of cigarette papers stuffed inside the envelope. He wrote on the first paper, "Deserted for the love of you."

Rocky promptly wrote back that she "shed tears of joy" over the gesture, while urging him to "keep his resolution to never smoke again." She proudly showed the cigarette papers to everyone and spread the news that Emmett had agreed to stop smoking. Soon

Cullen Higgins and Olive Smith on their wedding day, March 20, 1901. Courtesy Samantha Usnick.

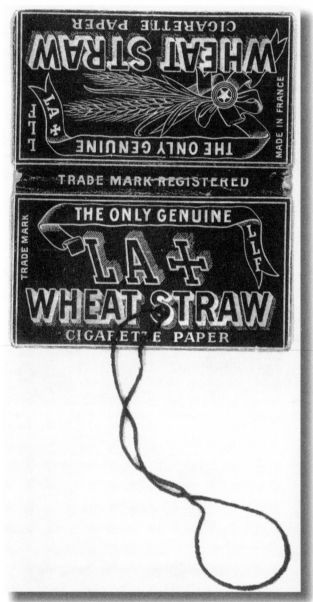

Emmett Johnson promised his fiancée, Rocky Higgins, that he would stop smoking, and as proof he mailed her his Wheat Straw cigarette papers, which she kept all her life. Courtesy Betty M. Giddens.

Rocky was approached by her sister, Ruby, and her future in-laws, Gladys and Ed Sims. With straight faces they presented her with a sack of tobacco to smoke with her cigarette papers. Reporting by letter to Emmett, Rocky teasingly announced her intention "to make them eat that tobacco next time I see them."

Rocky closed a subsequent letter with a promise: "If you haven't smoked yet I owe you 50 kisses." Emmett, having licked his habit, felt free to answer: "P.S. I haven't smoked yet. Send me those kisses." Rocky kept the Wheat Straw cigarette papers all of her life.

Rocky and Emmett were married at the home of Judge Cullen Higgins on Sunday evening, May 5, 1907. Emmett and Rocky were allotted the easternmost sections of the Johnson ranch, moving into a house on this portion of the big spread. Within a year of their marriage, a daughter named Rubinelle was born, followed by an infant son who died immediately, then another son named after his grandfather, W. A. Johnson.[23]

For a time it seemed that there might be another Higgins-Johnson wedding. Ruby Higgins was courted by Sidney Johnson, but Sid had qualities that Pink disliked. Although Ruby later found a spouse, she always held a soft spot for her first sweetheart. Sid married Ruth Smith, daughter of the late George Smith, who had preceded Billy Johnson as president of Snyder's First National Bank. Billy and Nannie Johnson presented the new couple with six sections of the ranch, and Sid built a comfortable story-and-a-half house. Sid and Ruth became the parents of a son, Weldon.[24]

With his family—and his fortune—expanding exponentially, Billy Johnson decided to erect a house worthy of a cattle baron, bank president, and grandfather. This magnificent residence was constructed a short distance east of the two-story frame ranch house, commanding the same splendid view from the mesa top. A sixteen-room manor was built of concrete blocks, which were fashioned of gravel and sand from nearby Ennis Creek. Billy Johnson hired a man for a dollar a day "and keep" to count the shovels of sand and cement to make certain the mixture was sound for the blocks and the mortar.[25]

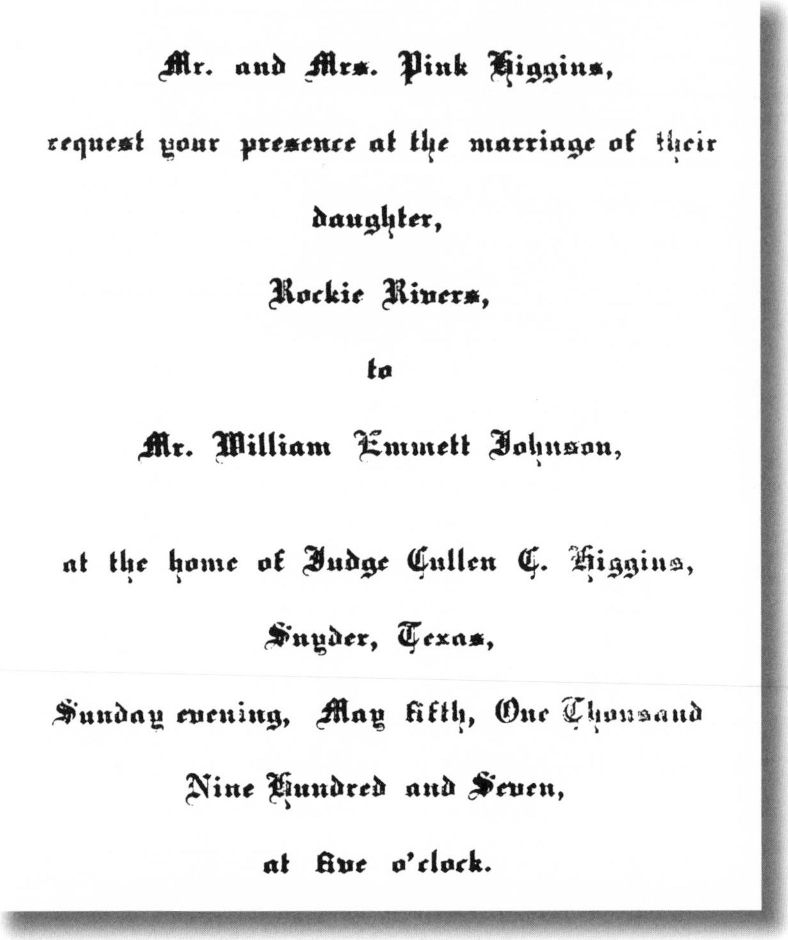

Mr. and Mrs. Pink Higgins,

request your presence at the marriage of their

daughter,

Rockie Rivers,

to

Mr. William Emmett Johnson,

at the home of Judge Cullen C. Higgins,

Snyder, Texas,

Sunday evening, May fifth, One Thousand

Nine Hundred and Seven,

at five o'clock.

Wedding invitation for Rockie Rivers Higgins and Emmett Johnson. (Despite the spelling on the wedding invitation, she usually spelled her name "Rocky," and sometimes "Rockye.") Courtesy Betty M. Giddens.

Wedding photo of Emmett Johnson and pretty Rocky Higgins. Courtesy Betty M. Giddens.

A master craftsman was employed to create a superb parquet floor in the parlor. To fasten the design, 1,500 pounds of nails were used to put the small oak pieces in place. The craftsman also hand-carved the oak banister on the big stairway. The second-floor landing served as a sitting room. A music room off the ground-floor parlor boasted an Edison record player. Also on the first floor was the bedroom for Billy and Nannie, and the only bathroom in the house was nearby. The Johnsons moved into their grand new home in 1910.

Gladys Johnson Sims enjoyed bringing her children to visit this spacious, beautifully furnished residence. Visits were less frequent to the large but utilitarian Sims ranch home. Beverly Sims remembered only two visits to her father's family home. Once she recalled walking across the dining room table—during a meal—to the welcoming arms of her grandfather Sims. On another visit she hit her big sister with a toy rake while playing in the yard.[26] Otherwise, most visits were to the home of her Johnson grandparents. It was harder to reach the Sims ranch, and Gladys naturally was more comfortable with her family than with her in-laws. Soon Gladys would bring her little girls to the Johnson home for extended stays, because her marriage to Ed was sinking into a quagmire of nasty accusations and counteraccusations.

Chapter 5

E. C. Sims vs. Gladys Sims

"[Ed is] without ambition or purpose in life other than to be down drunk or with other women . . . ."

Gladys Sims

"[Gladys] being unrestrained acquired habits of extravagance and of following her own ideas as to worldly pleasures without restraint."

Ed Sims

G ladys Sims was unhappy. She was unhappy with her husband, unhappy with her marriage, unhappy with herself. Gladys may have been physically mature when she married, but at fourteen she remained a girl, spoiled and headstrong and hot-tempered. At fourteen she did not yet know what she wanted out of life. Certainly she did not yet understand what she needed in a husband.

But she was a wife at fourteen, a mother at sixteen. At an age when she should still have been at school and attending parties, Gladys was unready for the responsibilities of marriage and motherhood. Frustrated and impatient for reasons she did not comprehend, Gladys at this point was incapable of creating a happy home.

With an unhappy, short-tempered wife, Ed Sims found himself in a perplexing situation. In a male-dominated society, many husbands made scant effort to coddle their wives. It is not known how hard Ed may have tried to please and pamper his young wife, but probably there was little he could have done to bring her happiness at this stage in her life. Ed later would swear that he "did all in his power . . . to render her life one of happiness . . . making special preparations for her comfort and welfare . . . ." Ed emphasized that "he continued at all times affectionate toward her . . . ."[1]

Ed did not find much response to all of the affection and special preparations he claimed to have lavished upon Gladys. She merely "was reasonably considerate" of Ed, despite his best efforts. A deeper problem, according to Ed, originated in her upbringing. Gladys, he explained, "was reared in her girl hood in a life of luxury, her parents being wealthy, and she being unrestrained acquired habits of extravagance and of following her own ideas as to worldly pleasures without restraint."[2]

Of course, Ed knew before the wedding that Gladys had been reared by wealthy parents, so any habit of extravagance that she brought to their marriage should not have been a total surprise. Regarding "her own ideas as to worldly pleasures without restraint,"[3] Gladys apparently engaged in extramarital affairs. But so did Ed.

Despite the joy their little girls brought to their household, there was growing acrimony between Ed and Gladys. Ed found life at home tense and unpleasant, and at some point he began to seek relief from a bottle. Ed "habitually became intoxicated with whiskey, wines, and other malt liquors," Gladys would accuse. According to her, Ed became a "profligate drunkard, . . . without ambition or purpose in life other than to be down drunk, or with other women than" his wife.[4]

On "several" occasions Gladys packed up her daughters and moved out of their Garza County ranch house into the splendid new home of her parents. After each of these separations Gladys returned to live with Ed. Soon, however, he would engage in "drinking, carousing and spreeing in a spinthrift [*sic*] and profligate manner," and Gladys again

The sixteen-room Johnson ranch house, built in 1910 of concrete blocks. Located twelve miles northeast of Snyder, this splendid house faces east. Photo by the author.

would depart for the Johnson ranch. Nannie awaited, ready to add fuel to the fire with criticism of Ed. "Gran had a lot to do" with the trouble between Ed and Gladys, insisted Beverly Sims Benson.[5]

But Gladys made her own contribution to the estrangement. In August 1913 Gladys took her little girls for a visit to her Mellard relatives in Presidio County. Gladys, Trix, and Beverly were accompanied by one of Ed's unmarried sisters. Ada McMeans was the only Sims daughter who had wed, although Dave had married in 1910. Sallie, who was five years older than Gladys, would marry in October 1913. Eva was twenty-one, but Belle and Georgia, at twelve and eight, were too young. So the "Miss Sims" who made the trip was either Eva or Sallie.[6]

R. T. Mellard had married Billy Johnson's older stepsister, Sallie, in 1871, and the couple had nine children. Most of the Mellard family migrated to Scurry County, and then later moved to Presidio County. R. T. had a ranch outside Marfa, and so did a son, Frank Courtney Mellard. Another son, twenty-five-year-old Garland, worked variously for his father and brother on their ranches, and for his aunt's husband, A. M. Avant, at his auto supply store in Marfa. Garland was a bachelor, and he and Gladys were "cousins" in name but not by blood.

In August 1913, while visiting Marfa and the Mellard ranches, Gladys often was alone with Garland. They rode off on horseback from R. T.'s ranch to get the mail. They went alone to "the car house" at Courtney's ranch and to the well house at R. T.'s ranch. They took automobile drives together. They were together at a dance. Ed was informed—probably by his sister—of this suspicious pairing. Ed immediately traveled to Marfa, where he was introduced to Garland at a dance hall.

The next day Garland drove Ed, Gladys, and their two girls to R. T.'s ranch. Garland and Gladys managed to slip into another room for a time, and then Garland drove back to town. The following morning Ed and his family began their journey home. Without doubt Ed quizzed Gladys jealously about Garland, not knowing that a furtive correspondence had been arranged between the "cousins." Garland wrote to Gladys through Mrs. Maude Marshall at Snyder, using Maude's name on the envelope.[7]

Somehow Ed found out about this secret correspondence. Ed and Billy Johnson developed a "stratagem" to intercept this mail, and they began reading Garland's letters. Illicit conduct between the two was confirmed, along with a plan to elope. Gladys even persuaded Garland to let her bring Trix and Beverly. One evening Billy Johnson and Ed loaded an unsuspecting Gladys, along with the two little girls, into a car and drove away from the Snyder square. Stopping at the outskirts of town, Ed and Billy confronted Gladys with the letters.

At first decrying her innocence, Gladys soon admitted guilt. With six-year-old Trix and four-year-old Beverly looking on in confusion, Gladys confessed to having sexual relations with Mellard on three occasions, relating specifics of time and place.

Long indulgent of his daughter, Billy Johnson snapped. Exploding with rage that had built up while he read the incriminating letters, he exclaimed that he would not bear such conduct. Furiously he threatened to kill Gladys. Probably reducing his granddaughters to tears, Billy quickly calmed down and drove back to the bank. Already it was nightfall, and the little girls were bedded down. During the long night Gladys pleaded with Ed, "assuring him that she would never again go astray and that if he would only take her back as his wife for her sake and the sake of her children, that she would be and remain unto him a true and dutiful and affectionate wife . . . ."[8]

Ed said that if Gladys "would remain faithful to him and demean herself as a lady," he would forgive her and extend "his best efforts to restore a happy state between them . . . ." But Ed was "greatly mortified in mind and heart," and his wife's infidelity "rankled and tortured him ever thereafter . . . ."[9]

Indeed, Ed threatened to kill Garland Mellard "on first sight," and a seething Billy Johnson said that if Ed failed to kill Mellard he would. Johnson arranged for mutual acquaintances to relay these threats to Mellard, along with a warning to stay away from Scurry County and anywhere else he might encounter Ed Sims. After receiving this warning Mellard prudently stayed away, and a year later he married another woman.

Gladys and the girls moved back to the Garza County ranch. But Ed now was perpetually alert and jealous. He suspected Gladys of having an affair with Ed Reifel of Scurry County in 1913. The next year he became convinced that Gladys had "illicit conduct with one Jim Edmonds . . . , lavishing her affections upon" him. At about the same time Gladys supposedly flirted with Lee Byrd, proposing an affair which he declined and reported to Ed or to someone who told Ed.[10] Lee Byrd may have exaggerated some remark or gesture from Gladys, so that he could brag to a friend, as men and boys always have done. But Ed felt disgraced and wounded, and he was ready to believe the worst about his straying wife.

His wife's infidelity may have provided Ed a certain self-granted freedom to pursue his own affairs, especially during Gladys's periodic absences. Mildred Girard, a girlhood friend of Gladys, had become a dressmaker, living with her mother in Dallas. Gladys sent for Mildred, intending that she would stay for several weeks and create dresses for herself, her daughters, and perhaps her mother and sister-in-law. But Mildred and Ed became attracted to each other. Gladys saw Ed "hug and kiss and caress" Mildred, and on occasion Ed and Mildred would drive off "on several mile trips." When Ed and Gladys traveled to the Fort Worth Stock Show, Ed insisted on going to Dallas for Mildred. He brought Mildred to the Stock Show "against the desires" of his wife. Gladys also believed that Ed bought a $900 diamond ring for Mildred.[11]

In Dallas, Mildred made dresses for Mrs. Drusilla Dorsey, a wealthy widow. Mrs. Dorsey's son, who lived in Colorado, had expressed interest in owning a ranch in West Texas that she would buy for him. Knowing that Mildred was from West Texas, Mrs. Dorsey asked her advice. Mildred told her she knew a "West Texas ranchman" who could be of help, and she contacted Ed about the matter in September 1915. Ed became excited about the prospect of brokering a ranch sale, as well as the opportunity to see Mildred. Anticipating a large fee, Ed located several possible properties for Mrs. Dorsey's consideration, and he kept her informed.

On Tuesday, February 8, 1916, Mrs. Dorsey set out for Post City in her seven-passenger Buick. Her entourage included her driver, her maid, and Mildred Girard, in the role of traveling companion and intermediary with Ed Sims. Mrs. Dorsey favored a leisurely pace, and roads were not very good. She stayed in the little town of Caddo the first night, and by the time she reached Stamford on Wednesday she was unwell. She summoned a local physician three times during the night, and he advised her to drive to Abilene and return to Dallas by train. On Thursday Mildred telephoned Ed, who drove to Stamford while Mrs. Dorsey proceeded to Abilene with her driver and maid. Ed and Mildred reunited in Stamford, then drove to Abilene in his car.[12]

The party stayed in Abilene's Grace Hotel. Mrs. Dorsey felt better and decided to return home by automobile, taking the curative waters at Mineral Wells en route. Ed left his car in Abilene and came along in the big Buick. In Mineral Wells the party checked into the Crazy Wells Hotel, visited the bathhouse, attended a silent movie after dinner, then returned to the hotel to watch a floor show. On the way back the party dined at Fort Worth's Metropolitan Hotel. In Dallas, before returning to her home, Mrs. Dorsey dropped off Ed and Mildred at the residence of Mildred and her mother.

"I never saw Mr. Sims again," stated Mrs. Dorsey. She discussed Ed's business proposals with her attorney. "He told me that, in his opinion, I had no use whatever for a ranch in west Texas, and on his advice, I at once abandoned the negotiations." Although Ed thereby lost a land sale commission, he had the consolation of a visit with Mildred.[13]

In November 1914 Ed sent Gladys and their daughters to the Johnson home, "intending that she should stay there, and not remain with him as husband and wife," explained Gladys. Gladys, of course, may have moved out on her own volition. Gladys and the girls brought all of their clothes, and most of their furniture and household goods, to the splendid house in Scurry County. Billy Johnson employed a governess-teacher to work with Trix and Beverly. Rubinelle, or "Dugie," the daughter of Emmett and Rocky, also was schooled at the ranch with her cousins.[14]

After Gladys and Nannie repeatedly denounced Ed's drinking and infidelities and other supposed shortcomings, Billy forgave his daughter her affair with Garland Mellard. Now reconciled, Billy and Gladys became worried about Ed's ability to manage the Garza County ranch. Gladys and Ed had "segregated" their property. Ed retained two sections, along with one section he had been given on the Sims home ranch. He kept eight cows, five saddle horses, one colt, his automobile, and a one-third interest in thirty OXO cows. (Ed's partnership in the OXO cattle probably was with his brother Kelly and either his father or his brother Lee Roy, and it is likely that this little herd had grazed on Ed's Garza County sections.) In order to protect his $25,000 investment, Billy Johnson became the trustee of Gladys's property.[15]

Ed was "notified not to come upon the Johnson premises; that if he does so, it is at his own peril . . . ." Ed took this threat seriously, but in practical terms it meant that he was cut off from his daughters. Ed managed a few "chance" encounters, but on these occasions he was able to speak only briefly to his girls. He became convinced that Gladys and her parents were poisoning Trix and Beverly against him. Trix seemed afraid of her father, and would barely speak to him, although Beverly remained affectionate. During an encounter with his girls in Snyder, Ed asked them to go on a trip with him for a few days. Trix refused to go, but Beverly liked the idea, and Ed promptly drove off with his youngest daughter. Gladys was upset, fearful that Ed might take Beverly out of the state, but three or four days later he delivered his little girl back to Snyder.[16]

Despite their constant difficulties, Gladys and Ed periodically reunited at the Garza County ranch. But these reconciliation attempts never lasted long. During one such attempt Gladys agreed to visit the Kent County home of Ed's brother and sister-in-law, Dave and Alma Sims. After a couple of days, however, Gladys said she was sick, and Dave took her to her father's home. According to Gladys, she remained in bed for four weeks, but Ed "never came to see her nor called her up

Standing, L to R, at the Johnson ranch house: Rubinelle "Dugie" Johnson, daughter of Emmett and Rocky; Beverly and Helen Trix Sims, daughters of Ed and Gladys. Courtesy Betty M. Giddens.

by phone to inquire for her condition . . . ." Finally Gladys and Ed visited the law offices of Judge Cullen Higgins and his current partner, W. W. Hamilton, to discuss filing a divorce suit. Instead they were advised to move back to Garza County, with their children and the governess, and try once more to reconcile. Early in 1916 Gladys, her daughters, and their governess united with Ed in Garza County. Within a few days, however, Ed received a phone call from Mildred Girard in Stamford. He drove off to pursue his real estate deal, and during the next several days Gladys telephoned and telegraphed "different stations between Stamford, Abilene and Dallas," at last locating Ed at Mildred's residence in Dallas. Gladys was furious, and she called a brother—probably Sid—to have him come to move them back to the Johnson ranch."[17]

Ed's departure triggered another visit by Gladys to the offices of Higgins and Hamilton. On February 8, 1916, the same date that the Dorsey entourage left Dallas, a divorce suit against Ed Sims was filed on behalf of Gladys Johnson Sims in the District Court of Scurry County. When the case came up on May 20, 1916, the law firm of Beall and Douthit, representing Ed Sims, contended that Gladys had not lived in Scurry County for the requisite six months. Beall and Douthit— J. H. Beall and Ellis Douthit—applied for the suit to be continued to the September term of the district court, and the continuance was granted. Beall and Douthit then filed a divorce suit, E. C. Sims vs. Gladys Sims, in the District Court of Garza County, and the case was scheduled for July 25, 1916.[18]

Ed's lawyers guided him in writing a new will. Anticipating "the pending separation of myself and wife Gladys Johnson Sims, pre Supposing a divorcement of such marriage," Ed and his attorneys crafted a three-page will "revoking any and all wills heretofore made by me." Ed's brother Kelly was named executor, along with his father and another brother. Ed bequeathed everything—including a $20,000 Aetna Life Insurance policy originally intended for his daughters—to Kelly. Although "entertaining a Strong fatherly love for my two girl children," Ed wrote them out of his will. He charged Kelly to provide for his daughters "should they at any time here after become in want

Main Street of Post City, looking east. The Algerita Hotel is the first building at right. Note the boulevard arrangement of Main Street. Courtesy Garza County Museum.

and in need of a Support," but he eliminated Trix and Beverly as beneficiaries of his will. No matter how angry Ed was that the Johnson
family was trying to turn his daughters against him, no matter how
comfortably Billy Johnson could maintain Trix and Beverly, it is difficult to countenance a father eliminating his young children from his
estate. This will was signed by Ed and witnessed by his attorneys on
May 17, 1916.[19]

On June 8 Gladys's lawyers obtained a restraining order from
Judge John B. Thomas of the Thirty-ninth Judicial District in Haskell.
Ed was prohibited from taking custody of his daughters. "A good deal
of excitement and bitter feeling was aroused on account of this injunc-
tion," reported an area newspaper, adding that "various other mis-
haps and unpleasantness" ensued. Less than three weeks later, Beall
and Douthit pleaded Ed's case before Judge Thomas, who modified
his order of June 8. Ed was permitted to have custody of the girls
for ten days beginning immediately, then again on alternate ten-day
periods until public schools opened in Snyder in September. Gladys
then would have custody of the children "until the further order of
the court . . . ." Exchange of the girls every ten days between the war-
ring parents was ordered to take place at the Manhattan Hotel on the
square in Snyder.[20]

Nearly fifty witnesses were summoned to the July 25 divorce
hearing in Post City. Ed Reifel and Lee Byrd and Jim Edmonson were
subpoenaed, while depositions were taken from Garland Mellard and
Mrs. Drusilla Dorsey. By Monday, July 24, witnesses had gathered at
Post City, many checking into the Algerita Hotel. Hard feelings had
mounted steadily, and everyone brought weapons. Little was done to
conceal the provocative fact "that each side was well armed, having
pistols, Winchesters, and shotguns of almost every description."[21]

Packing an automatic pistol, Gladys fumed with barely suppressed
anger. In the upstairs hallway of the Algerita Hotel she encountered Gee McMeans, a former lawman and an experienced gunhand.
McMeans and Gladys both had married into the Sims family in 1905,
but Gee remained fiercely loyal to Ed and to the rest of his wife's clan.
Gladys and Gee began arguing, then angrily produced their pistols.

The Algerita Hotel, scene of the 1916 confrontation between Gladys Sims and Gee McMeans, and their well-armed supporters. Later McMeans tried to goad an unarmed Harrison Hamer into a fight in the hotel. Photo by Karon O'Neal.

Doors opened and members of both factions witnessed a stand-off, with Gladys and McMeans brandishing handguns while shouting at each other. Someone called down to the lobby, and within moments Sheriff E. J. Robinson and officer J. E. Cash hustled upstairs. Officer Cash beseeched Gladys to surrender her gun, but she adamantly refused. When Cash tried to seize her weapon a scuffle broke out. The automatic went off and the bullet narrowly missed Cash. Gladys's gun clattered to the floor and Sheriff Robinson quickly seized it.

Tension crackled in a hallway crowded with armed partisans. But the sheriff and other peacemakers calmed members of both factions, then persuaded everyone to surrender their weapons. A small arsenal was collected. The guns of one faction were secured in the First National Bank across the street, while weapons of the opposing group were placed in a nearby office. The next morning, as everyone crowded into the courtroom, Sheriff Robinson searched the men for concealed weapons. Miss Annie Rodgers, specially deputized for this task, examined Gladys and the female witnesses.

The court proceedings were routine. Cullen Higgins contended that the divorce case should be returned to Scurry County, where Gladys had filed early in the year. Ed's attorneys countered that Post City was the rightful trial location, since the couple had made their home in Garza County. Judge W. R. Spencer suspended the divorce hearing, pending action of the Scurry County court in September. By that evening Gladys and Ed, along with their lawyers and friends— and an impressive collection of firearms—had left town.

The rest of the summer passed without notable incident. In September the two teams of lawyers presented forty-five pages of arguments and documents to Judge Thomas in his chambers at the Scurry County Courthouse.[22] The material read by Judge Thomas was identical to the case filed in Garza County. In addition, the depositions and documents of Garland Mellard and Mrs. Dorsey totaled nearly twenty pages. All of the arguments and testimonies, the depositions and documents, revealed a painful account of a mismatched man and

On July 25, 1916, the First National Bank of Post became a repository for guns confiscated from men—and women—entering the courtroom for the divorce hearing of Ed and Gladys Sims. Photo by the author.

Garza County's first courthouse was built on the north side of Main Street in 1908. In 1916 the divorce hearing of Ed and Gladys Sims was held here—after everyone was searched for weapons before entering the courtroom. This structure was replaced by a much larger courthouse in 1923. Courtesy Garza County Museum.

woman tormenting each other year after year. Love turned to loathing, and Ed and Gladys struck at each other in mean-spirited efforts to wound and humiliate. The divorce was granted, at last ending the long strife between Ed and Gladys—legally.

Chapter 6

Storm Clouds

"Gladys adored Frank Hamer."

Beverly Sims Benson

By the time that her divorce from Ed Sims was finalized, Gladys had found the love of her life. Frank Hamer already was famous as a Texas Ranger and deadly gunman, and he would prove a formidable ally for the Johnson family.

Francis Augustus Hamer was born on March 17, 1884. He was the second of eight children born to Frank and Lou Emma Francis Hamer. A former cavalryman, the senior Hamer had served in Texas as a farrier with Col. Ranald Mackenzie and his crack Fourth Cavalry Regiment. Following his discharge, the young veteran married a Texas girl, and they raised their family in adjoining San Saba and Llano counties. Young Francis—also called Frank or Pancho—learned his way around his father's blacksmith shop. He grew up riding and roping, fishing and hunting, and he became an excellent shot. While reveling in the outdoor life of the Texas Hill Country, he was a bright student in the rural school at his home village of Oxford, about eight miles south of Llano. (Later Hamer liked to joke that he was the only Texas Ranger with an Oxford education.) During emotional camp meeting revival services young Frank developed the ambition to become a preacher.[1]

But in 1900 the aspiring parson clashed with a murderous land-owner named Dan McSwain. Sixteen-year-old Frank and twelve-year-old Harrison contracted to sharecrop one of McSwain's farms. When McSwain discovered that Frank was an expert shot, he offered the young sharpshooter $200 to kill a rival rancher. Frank adamantly refused, and McSwain, fearing that he would reveal the murder scheme, attacked with a shotgun. The second blast slammed into Frank's back, and he would carry some of the shot the rest of his life. Despite his wounds, Frank nicked McSwain with a revolver slug before being carried to safety by his brother Harrison. After his wounds healed, Frank deliberately rode to the McSwain Ranch and killed McSwain in a revolver duel. The vision of Rev. F. A. Hamer evaporated before the reality of temperament and a hard land. Frank Hamer was a rough soul who never would turn the other cheek. The aggressive combativeness that would propel Hamer throughout his lifetime first asserted itself when he was sixteen. Any man who tried to fight Frank Hamer, with fists or guns, would immediately find himself assailed by a fierce adversary. Late in life he told a reporter that he had been involved in fifty-two shootings, and that he had suffered twenty-three wounds. "Several of those bullets are in me yet," including shot from his first gunplay.[2]

Not long after the trouble with Dan McSwain, Frank and Harrison left home to find work as cowboys. In 1905, while Frank was cowboying on a ranch near Fort Stockton, two rustlers stole horses from the spread. Hamer, now an imposing six-three and 195 pounds, tracked down the stock thieves and captured them at Winchester point. A few months later he apprehended another rustler. Relishing the satisfaction of bringing criminals to justice, in 1906 twenty-two-year-old Frank Hamer enlisted as a private in Company C of the Texas Rangers.[3] Headquartered in Alpine, Company C was commanded by the legendary Captain John H. Rogers. Along the border Private Hamer learned and embraced a rough brand of law enforcement from the Texas Rangers.

In 1908 Hamer was recommended for the post of city marshal
of Navasota, a town plagued by rowdy troublemakers and racial conflict. Marshal Hamer vigorously exerted control, although an anti-
Hamer faction developed in town. While in Navasota Hamer married,
but within six months his bride drowned at a Sunday School picnic.
Always taciturn, Hamer said little about the tragedy, but clearly he
was reluctant to commit to another marriage.[4]

After more than two years of battling the lawless element in Navasota, Hamer was hired as a special officer by the mayor of Houston.
With Mexico torn by revolution, in 1915 Hamer rejoined the Rangers
and again was assigned to border duty. To the growing list of Hamer's
battles as a lawman were added tales of violent encounters with ban-
dits and smugglers. Frank Hamer became regarded as "a power for
law and order" and "a terror to the lawless," according to his friend
and admirer, Ranger historian Walter Prescott Webb.[5] In 1916, when
the Texas Cattle Raisers Association asked the Texas Rangers to
detach a man to help them apprehend rustlers in West Texas, Hamer
was commissioned a Special Texas Ranger and detailed to assist the
association.

It was in this capacity that Ranger Hamer visited his brother
Harrison, who was employed at the Johnson ranch. Frank was introduced to Gladys, and she was powerfully impressed. "He was daring
and handsome," Gladys told Frank's biographer. According to her
daughter Beverly, "Gladys adored Frank Hamer." And the attrac-
tion was mutual. Gladys was petite and pretty and far more mature
than she had been as a bride a decade earlier. The big Ranger called
her "Bunch"—short for "Honey Bunch"—and he addressed letters to
Gladys as "H. B."[6]

Frank Hamer's growing attachment to Gladys—and to her
family—would lead to one of the explosive events that punctuated
his life. Perhaps Hamer, with vast experience in homicidal conflicts,
sensed the oncoming danger that threatened to erupt into violence. But
most people in the area probably thought that blood feuds belonged to

West Texas of the nineteenth century and ignored the gathering storm clouds of another clash.

Like other Americans early in the twentieth century, West Texans now enjoyed Coca Cola and ice cream parlors and toothpaste in a tube. In the fall of 1908 Henry Ford began manufacture of the first Model T automobile, a mass-produced, simple, sturdy vehicle that contrasted sharply with the hand-made luxury autos that could be purchased only by the wealthy. The "Tin Lizzie" or "flivver" soon was priced at $290, and by 1914 every second automobile that was manufactured in the United States was a Ford. The rugged Model T was readily repaired by farmers and ranchers, who were accustomed to repairing windmills and machinery. By the second decade of the twentieth century automobiles were commonplace on the streets of Snyder and Post. Railroad tracks finally reached Snyder in 1908, Post late in 1910. Vaudeville companies and theatrical troupes now could come to town, and an opera house was built on the Snyder square. Silent movies could be shipped to Snyder and Post, where the Garza Theater opened in 1916.

There was a spirit of the modern, a sense of an exciting new century, among Americans—including West Texans. But in West Texas, frontier conditions were just a single generation in the past. Indeed, many West Texas pioneers were no more than middle-aged, and their attitudes remained rooted in the frontier of their youth. Billy Johnson, a teenaged pioneer cattleman of Scurry County, now was at the height of his prominence and power in Snyder. Dave Sims, one of the first ranchers in Kent County, commanded respect and deference as the patriarch of a large family. Sharing the backgrounds and outlooks of their successful husbands, Nannie Johnson and Laura Belle Sims were strong-minded forces for tradition within their respective communities. West Texans such as these inexorably were moving toward the new, but their thinking and instincts were still shaped by the old.

In 1913 Pink Higgins died of a heart attack at his ranch house. The old feudist had not killed anyone in eleven years, and his passing must have reinforced the impression that blood feuds had been relegated to

Billy Standifer's headstone proclaimed that
he was "KILLED BY PINK HIGGINS." Photo by
Karon O'Neal.

Pink Higgins late in life, wearing laced-up
boots on a snowy day in West Texas. It is
believed that he is standing beside the board-
and-batten house he built on his Catfish
Ranch in 1907. Courtesy Betty M. Giddens.

the frontier past. But the attitudes and traditions that triggered feuding still lurked close to the surface in West Texas.

Although Pink Higgins was dead, there were younger men—dangerous men—in the area, men such as Will Luman; the Rasberry brothers, Lee and Alfred; and Joshua and Si Bostick, father and son. In earlier years these hair-triggered gunmen would have been willing participants in the Regulator-Moderator War or the Horrell-Higgins Feud or any of the other murderous clashes of the nineteenth century. But the malignant environment they helped to recreate, the poison they unleashed in 1915–16, was embraced so readily by other West Texans that the civilized veneer of the twentieth century vanished in a hateful explosion of gunfire. The violent past of the 1800s proved prologue for the second decade of the twentieth century.

Will "Dutch" Luman was a reckless cowboy in his twenties who seemed like a throwback to a more violent era. "I was just a little, chunky, cotton-headed, heavy-set kid, and my daddy always called me Dutch." The seven Luman sisters adored and spoiled their only brother. But Dutch developed an explosive temper and a combative nature, quick to use his fists—or a gun. Through ceaseless practice he became a superb marksman with a Winchester. At his father's ranch near Verbena, in eastern Garza County, Dutch targeted a hackberry tree. Drilling the target with one rifle bullet after another, Dutch finally killed the hackberry tree.[7]

"That used to be a wonderful country," reminisced Dutch Luman. "Of course there weren't many people lived in that country in those days. It was all open and had no fences." Dutch was raised with old-fashioned virtues. "My mother and daddy taught me all my life that my word was my bond," he remarked in old age. "If I tell a man something, I'll sure stand behind it, come hell or high water."[8] Dutch also absorbed the frontiersman's absolute loyalty to family, and he would stand behind his kin, come hell or high water.

One of his kin was a hard-luck cowboy, Lee Rasberry, who married a Luman sister. Lee and Mary Rasberry, along with their two children, lived in poverty in Kent County, while Dutch and other family members offered what help they could. In 1914 Rasberry was accused, on the skimpiest of circumstantial evidence, of killing and butchering a cow on O Bar O range near his shack. He was convicted and sentenced to two years in prison.[9]

Will Luman was incensed at the injustice he felt had been perpetrated upon his brother-in-law. In the Kent County Courthouse in Clairemont, Luman overheard Nick Bilby, part owner of the O Bar O grumble "that the way he done fellows like Lee Rasberry wasn't to go to court with him, but was to put a rope around their neck and hang them to a cottonwood limb." Luman charged Bilby, and after they "fought all over the room," the battered rancher had to be carried to his hotel. Later the O Bar O range boss, Dock Howell, tried to pull a revolver on Luman. But Dutch quickly leveled his Winchester, and Howell had to beg to save his life. "My God, think of my wife and babies."[10]

After only a few months in the penitentiary, Lee Rasberry was pardoned by Governor James A. Ferguson.[11] But Rasberry seethed with bitterness. Reportedly he wrote to two men, Joshua Bostick and Sidney Johnson (a rancher and constable who was the younger brother of W. A. Johnson), demanding that each man pay him $250 because of their role in sending him to prison. When the money was not forthcoming, Rasberry found Constable Johnson in the Riverdale Community, administered a beating, then collected $250.[12]

Joshua Bostick had no intention of surrendering $250 or taking a beating. After receiving threats from Rasberry, the rancher took the initiative. On October 27, 1915, Bostick sought out Rasberry in Rotan and shot him to death on the street.

Will Luman wanted blood vengeance, and so did Alfred Rasberry, Lee's brother. Luman had additional incentive: his friend, Gee McMeans, had told him that Bostick was hired to kill him by Nick Bilby, who sought revenge for the courthouse beating he had absorbed from Luman.[13] Bostick was scheduled to stand trial in Roby on Monday, March 6, 1916. Suspecting that he was being hunted, Bostick decided to come in from his ranch on Friday, March 3. Bostick took the precaution of using a roundabout trail, and he also brought along his fifteen-year-old daughter Lizzie, perhaps thinking—incorrectly— that he would not be killed in her presence. They traveled in a two-horse hack, and Bostick carried a rifle.

At mid-morning the Bosticks were intercepted by Will Luman and Alfred Rasberry. Bostick seized his rifle and descended from the vehicle. Luman later testified that Bostick got off one shot. Luman pulled his Winchester and slipped off his horse, but the frightened animal bolted, throwing his rider. Luman scrambled to his feet, working his rifle with practiced expertise. He drilled Bostick five times. Under oath Luman later would admit, "I am counted a pretty good shot with a Winchester, a crack shot."[14]

Riddled with five bullets, Bostick died on the spot. Fearing for her life, Lizzie Bostick picked up her father's rifle and threatened to shoot Luman and Rasberry if they approached her. Lizzie later admitted that she did not know how to fire the gun but her father's killers did not know that. Luman and Rasberry rode away without harming Lizzie. While the killing appeared premeditated, if they had murdered Bostick in cold blood, as they were accused, why did they not also murder the only eyewitness? Perhaps Bostick did try to fight back, so that Luman and Rasberry believed that they could successfully plead self-defense.

After they rode off, Lizzie placed her father's hat over his face. She pulled from his pockets his watch and other valuables. After half an hour, with no passersby on the lonely trail, Lizzie drove off to find help. She reached a house about two miles from the killing site, and a telephone call was made to the Fisher County sheriff's office in Roby.[15]

A manhunt soon resulted in the capture of Rasberry, but Luman escaped into New Mexico. On March 8, 1916, Luman (in absentia) and Rasberry were indicted for murder. Rasberry was tried, convicted, and sentenced to twenty-five years in prison. His lawyers appealed the verdict, and the court of appeals eventually reversed the decision, which led to a new trial, scheduled for September 1917. Will Luman, meanwhile, periodically slipped back home to see his wife, children, and other family members. But officers finally caught Luman at Post

City in May 1917, arresting the fugitive in time to bring him to trial with Rasberry.[16]

Often used as a special prosecutor, Cullen Higgins was appointed special prosecuting attorney against Will Luman. In September 1917, Higgins, the district attorney, and the defense attorneys agreed upon a change of venue, from Fisher County to Haskell County. Luman's trial, in December 1917, resulted in a hung jury. Another trial was scheduled for May 13, 1918. While between trial appearances, Luman was free on bail.

Within a period of just over four months—October 27, 1915, to March 3, 1916—Lee Rasberry and, in retaliation, Joshua Bostick, were gunned down in the violent style of the Old West. These shooting deaths seemed to unleash the murderous forces of frontier-style blood feuding. Before the year was out another shooting triggered an explosion of vicious retributions. In the poisoned atmosphere of the region, the legal expertise of Cullen Higgins placed his life in jeopardy, while Billy Johnson, despite his wealth and prominence, found himself stalked by gunmen. The lethal skills of Will Luman were in demand, and his friend and fellow gun hand, Gee McMeans, would be swept—perhaps willingly—into the deadly current of events as champion of the Sims family. Si Bostick, a cattle thief and son of Joshua Bostick, hired out as an assassin, and so did other reckless men. It was as if there was no law, no lawmen, no courts. Mary Luman Rasberry and Mrs. Joshua Bostick were not the only women in the region who would become bereaved widows.

Chapter 7

Tragedy in Snyder

"You see what you have done. I am unarmed."

Ed Sims, after being shot by his ex-wife.

The divorce of Ed and Gladys Sims was finalized in September 1916. Soon afterward Ed married Mildred Girard, the dressmaker from Dallas, but he continued to find it difficult to arrange custody time with his daughters. He stated flatly that Gladys and her parents were "prejudicing his children against him." While little Beverly retained warm feelings for her father, nine-year-old Trix clearly was becoming hardened against Ed. He bitterly expressed his resentment, and Cullen Higgins later described "a long series of insulting conduct" by Ed against Gladys and other members of the Johnson family. Relations between Ed and the Johnsons worsened. [1]

The frequent divorces of contemporary society produce countless conflicts and immeasurable antagonisms between parents over child custody. At least the fact that this wrenching problem is commonplace today is an initial step toward accommodation. In 1916 divorce was uncommon, and to the social stigma of legal division was added the unexpected pain of separation from children. In the months following their acrimonious divorce, Gladys and Ed were jealous of the time the other parent spent with their children.

Ed remained persona non grata on Johnson property. But in November Beverly turned seven, and Ed decided to give her a Shetland pony. He arranged to meet Beverly at the gate to the Johnson Ranch. Ed drove up with a tiny red Shetland pony in the back seat. Careful not to cross the fence line, Ed passed the pony through to his little girl. Beverly named her gift horse "Red Bird." [2]

Ed managed to arrange a Christmas season visit which would begin on Saturday, December 16, 1916. Gladys always was reluctant to cooperate, and she and her mother must have made Trix and Beverly apprehensive about the upcoming visit with Ed and his new wife. Ed, too, was apprehensive. When he drove to Snyder to pick up his daughters he brought along two handguns and a rifle.

Ed arrived in Snyder on Friday. Billy Johnson was in town late, and about 9:30 that evening he encountered Ed at the Warren Drug Store on the square. Perhaps Ed had been drinking; certainly he was on edge and filled with animosity over the events of recent months. While bystanders watched in surprise, Ed vehemently berated Johnson, as well as his absent wife, for trying to turn Trix and Beverly against their father. Furiously he pulled one of his handguns on his former father-in-law. [3]

Deputy Sheriff Sam Casstevens hastily intervened, seizing both pistols from Ed Sims. Unaccustomed to such brazen treatment, Billy Johnson left the premises with his longtime friend Robert Curnutte, vice president of the bank. Curnutte accompanied Billy on the dark drive to the Johnson ranch. Shaken and angry, Billy aroused the house when he arrived, and he and Curnutte related the actions and threats of Ed Sims. Billy's family was appalled that their patriarch had been publicly upbraided—that the despised Ed Sims had the gall to threaten W. A. Johnson with a gun.

Gladys and Sidney were livid. Years of angry conflict with Ed had fueled hatred, and Gladys's loathing increased after their divorce because of the clash over child custody. Probably her fury was inflamed by the paradox of jealousy over the remarriage of her ex-husband and

Lee Rasberry, shot to death in the growing climate of violence. Courtesy Jon Bratta.

her ex-friend. It was infuriating that Ed and his new wife would take Trix and Beverly from her, even temporarily. For Ed then to insult and pull a gun on her father triggered the lethal animosity that welled within her. Sidney, always her closest sibling—in temperament as well as age—had commiserated with her over every marital hurt until he, too, detested Ed. Ed's public humiliation of Sid's father—at the point of a gun—was an affront to the Johnson family. The incident in the drugstore was too much for Sid to bear. Sid and Gladys were alike in their vindictive resolve to avenge the family honor, to deal with Ed with finality.

The next morning Sid brought along a pump-action shotgun when he drove into town with his father and Robert Curnutte. Sid placed the loaded weapon inside his father's bank. Back at the ranch, Gladys unhappily helped her daughters pack for their trip, but she was in no hurry to bring them to Snyder.

During the morning Ed Sims located Sheriff W. A. Merrill, asking the officer to drive to the Johnson ranch and bring the girls into Snyder. Sheriff Merrill, aware of the previous night's incident, notified Ed that he was not to carry handguns in Snyder unless he was on official business as a deputy sheriff of Garza County. The sheriff refused to drive to the ranch, but sought out Billy Johnson and requested that Trix and Beverly be brought into Snyder and turned over to their father. Johnson agreed to call Gladys at the ranch, but he was nervous about a possible confrontation. Although Billy may not have known about whatever deadly plans Gladys and Sid may have concocted, he had seen their angry reaction to the drugstore incident, and Johnson was sufficiently concerned to urge Sheriff Merrill to "be present and try to keep down trouble." The sheriff had seen enough to realize that the situation was potentially explosive, and he asked City Marshal O. P. "Pack" Wolf to be on the alert.

Complying with the sheriff's request, Johnson telephoned his ranch and instructed Gladys to bring Trix and Beverly into town. It was about twenty minutes until noon, and Gladys said she would arrive about 12:30 and park in front of the First National Bank.

Snyder's square, always busy on Saturdays, was even more crowded than usual with Christmas shoppers. The big open area around the courthouse was filled with teams of horses and the wagons and buggies they were hitched to, while automobiles were parked in front of commercial buildings around he square's perimeter.

At about noon Ed Sims, with Sheriff Merrill and a friend in the car, drove to the north side of the square and parked in front of the First National Bank. Ed and the sheriff stepped out of the car to wait for Gladys to arrive. Sid Johnson restlessly had left the bank and was sitting in his nearby automobile. When Sheriff Merrill spotted Sid, he walked over and asked him to go inside the bank. Sid complied, re-entering his father's bank—where his shotgun stood.

At half past twelve Gladys drove onto the square and parked near the bank. Sheriff Merrill and Ed returned to the Sims auto, and Ed maneuvered to within twenty feet of Gladys's car. While City Marshal Wolf watched alertly from the sidewalk, Sheriff Merrill and Ed again stepped out, then walked over to Gladys's vehicle. The sheriff stood beside the left front fender. Also on the driver's side, Ed leaned inside the back to kiss his daughters.

Gladys sat tensely in the driver's seat, fuming aloud that she had brought the girls but would not make them go, and Trix and Beverly took their cue from their mother. When Ed asked his daughters where their suitcases were, they tearfully replied that the bags were beside them in the back seat, but they would not go.

"Oh, yes," insisted Ed, "you must go with me."

Reaching deep into the car, Ed drew out a suitcase and set it on the running board. As the girls cried that they were not going, Ed grasped Beverly and tried to pull her out of the back seat. Gladys reacted ferociously, seizing her ever-present automatic and, reaching across Beverly, triggered three rounds rapid-fire.[4]

The first slug hit Ed's hat brim, "for I saw the fur fly," stated Sheriff Merrill. Then the bullets began to strike Ed.

"_ _ _ _ _ _ _ you," cursed Ed, clutching for the gun. Gladys got off a fourth shot before her pistol dropped behind the front seat. Sher-

Scurry County's new courthouse in 1912. Courtesy Scurry County Museum.

iff Merrill hurried to pull Ed aside, but the wounded man staggered away from the car. A flesh wound produced blood on his shirt front, while another slug had entered his lower left leg.

"You see what you have done," blurted Ed. Neither of the wounds was life-threatening, but he was stunned and confused. "I am unarmed."[5]

With all eyes on Ed, Sheriff Merrill and Marshal Wolf failed to see Sidney Johnson emerge from the bank with his shotgun. Sid leveled the deadly weapon and triggered a loud blast. The load of buckshot caught Ed beneath his right shoulder blade, hurling him onto his back.

Sid pumped another round into the chamber, but Sheriff Merrill leaped onto the sidewalk and seized the shotgun. The sheriff handed the weapon to Marshal Wolf, while Sidney murmured that "no man can curse my sister and her children" and "you cannot shoot and do around here like you can at Post City."[6]

Billy Johnson scurried outside and hustled his granddaughters into the bank. Beverly, the only participant who remained alive while this book was being written, recalls nothing of the shooting. At ninety-eight she recounted to the author with clarity and vivid detail events that preceded the death of her father. But mercifully the memory of her mother shooting her father, who then was finished off by Uncle Sidney, was blacked out: psychologists cited "dissociative amnesia" and "repressed memory" and even "post traumatic stress disorder" to the author. Beverly's first recollection of the tragic event is of her grandfather carrying her into the boardroom of the bank.[7]

Beverly and Trix did not see their father carried into Thompson's Drug Store by Sheriff Merrill and a few other men. While a crowd surged to the scene, the sheriff led the transfer of the wounded man into the nearby drugstore, located almost directly in front of Gladys's parked automobile.

Ed still was breathing. He was placed on a table in the back room of the drug store, and Dr. W. R. Johnson was summoned. (Although Dr. Johnson was not related to Billy Johnson, he was a friend of the family.) When Dr. Johnson hurried into the makeshift hospital room, Ed was struggling for breath, and moments later he died. The corpse was carried to an undertaker's office on the west side of the square, where Dr. Johnson and another physician conducted a post-mortem examination. The doctors ruled that both bullet wounds were superficial, while death had been inflicted by the shotgun charge. Justice of the Peace D. F. Wilson announced an examining trial for Monday afternoon, then placed Sidney Johnson under a $5,000 bond, which was posted by his father.

Many relatives and friends of Ed Sims traveled south to Snyder when they heard of the killing. His body was prepared for burial at the undertaking parlor, then taken to Post City, where stunned family members arranged funeral services.

At one-thirty on Monday afternoon, the office of Justice D. W. Wilson was packed. Judge Cullen Higgins represented Sidney and Gladys, while the State of Texas was represented by County Attorney W. W. Weems and by J. Henry Beall, a former district judge from Sweetwater. The lengthiest testimony was given by Sheriff Merrill, who thoroughly explained the Saturday morning negotiations as well as the shooting. "As quick as I heard the first shot I jumped right in between them and reached over," related the sheriff, "I don't know whether I struck her hand or not."[8]

Indictments were handed down, but Justice Wilson granted bail for Sidney for $20,000 and Gladys for $8,000. "The bonds were immediately posted," reported the *Snyder Signal*, which published the testimony of the examining trial.

"I am very much in sympathy with the Johnsons," emphasized bank vice-president Robert Curnutte during his testimony, "and with the defendants in this case." Curnutte's support was community-wide, as described by the *Snyder Signal*. "The Johnsons are a pioneer family and are among our most substantial citizenship. They own vast property interests here, being extensively interested in farming and ranching. W. A. Johnson is President of the First National Bank, and is an honorable, upright man. Sidney Johnson and Mrs. Sims have been reared here and have hosts of friends."[9]

Prosecution attorneys were justifiably concerned about the "hosts of friends" around Scurry County who supported Sidney and Gladys. The prosecution sought to have the trials moved away from Scurry County, contending that it was impossible to seat an impartial jury in Snyder. Most potential jurors had read the testimony of the examining trial in the *Snyder Signal*. In case anyone had missed the newspaper account, a circular containing the testimony was printed and distributed throughout the region. Furthermore, the Johnson family and Ed Sims were related to many members of the jury pool in Scurry County.

District Judge Warren Beall heard these arguments on June 7, 1917, in Snyder. Judge Beall ruled that, in the interests of impartiality, a change of venue was necessary. Gladys would be tried at Lamesa, seat of Dawson County to the west, while Sidney would stand trial at Baird in Callahan County, twenty miles east of Abilene. Bail for Sidney for the second round of legalities was set at $12,500, and among his eight sureties were his father, his brother Emmett, noted pioneer J. Wright Mooar, and a peace officer of ascendant reputation, Frank Hamer.[10]

Hamer now was Sidney's brother-in-law. After years of stress and violence Hamer found himself again ready for the warmth of feminine companionship. Embroiled in the most troubled period of her life, Gladys found the big Texas Ranger to be a tower of strength. Despite her pending murder trial in Lamesa, Frank and Gladys decided to marry.

The couple journeyed by train to New Orleans, where they wed on May 12, 1917. Frank was thirty-two, a widower, while Gladys desperately needed stability. After their return to the Johnson ranch, Frank became stepfather to the girls, functioning as a loyal and protective parent. Beverly called him "Daddy" and was devoted to him, but Trix maintained a certain reserve.[11]

The north side of the Snyder square, from a 1911 postcard. Cullen Higgins occupied upstairs offices in the First National Bank building on the corner. The double-parked car is about where Ed Sims double-parked on December 16, 1916, behind his ex-wife's car. Gladys shot him from her car, then Sid came from the bank and finished Ed with a shotgun. Courtesy Scurry County Museum, Snyder, Texas.

Frank Hamer, sitting tall in the saddle on a favorite horse, Bugler. Author's collection.

Frank Hamer now was a member of the Johnson family, at home in the big ranch house. In the troubled wake of the shooting death of Ed Sims, Hamer was a welcome reinforcement for the Johnson family—a proven warrior, one of the deadliest gunmen in Texas. The Johnsons soon would need his lethal expertise.

Chapter 8

The Search for Revenge

"Can vengeance be pursued further than death?"

Romeo and Juliet

". . . then thou shalt give life for life, eye for eye, tooth for tooth, hand for hand, foot for foot, burning for burning, wound for wound, stripe for stripe."

Exodus 21:23–25

E d Sims was buried in the Post City Cemetery on Sunday, December 17, the day after he was murdered. "The funeral was attended by a large crowd of people," reported the *Snyder Signal*.[1] Ed's loved ones made up a significant portion of those in attendance, because he was the first member of his immediate family to die. The youngest of the ten siblings, Georgia, was twelve.

Dave and Laura Belle Sims had not lost any of their ten children to illness, a tribute to good genes and a healthy outdoor life. The death of one or more children was a sad but common trauma to parents of the era, but Dave and Laura Belle had been spared this tragedy. Now, the fifty-nine-year-old father and fifty-one-year-old mother had lost their oldest son. Tall and handsome, Ed had been gunned down on a public street in view of his daughters. At thirty-two the beloved son and brother was wrenched from his close-knit family. Soon a large stone monument was placed over Ed's grave. His name and the dates of his birth and death were cited, and a carefully selected sentiment throbbed with meaning:

> Our precious one from us has gone,
> A voice we loved is stilled,
> A place is vacant in our home,
> Which never can be filled.

Such a devastating loss cried out for retribution, for Old Testament vengeance. On the weekend of Ed's death, a contingent of his kinsmen and friends came to Snyder to deliver the body to Post City. Feelings were ugly over the killing, and Sheriff Merrill was alarmed by the threats he overheard. He wired Governor James Ferguson, requesting "two experienced rangers . . . to remain through Christmas holidays." Ranger Captain J. M. Fox sent word that two of his men were on the way. Rangers John D. White and A. G. Beard soon arrived, and Sheriff Merrill managed to keep them in Snyder through the March term of the District Court.[2]

There were rumors that gunmen had been hired to kill Billy Johnson, and that Frank Hamer, now acting as Johnson's bodyguard, also was a target. A man named W. G. Clark later claimed to have been offered $4,000 to assassinate Johnson. Clark also implicated T. A. Morrison, while other sources—and future events—named H. E. Phillips, Bob Higdon, Si Bostick, and Gee McMeans.[3]

McMeans appears to have been the point man for the Sims faction. Family patriarch Dave Sims is not known ever to have engaged in gunplay, and at nearly sixty years of age apparently he was too old to try to become a shootist. But he must have wanted revenge for the murder of his oldest son, and just as surely his wife, the redoubtable Laura Belle, also hoped for retribution. Gee McMeans, their

Ed Sims was buried in the Post City Cemetery. He is the first member of his large immediate family to die, and the sentiment engraved on his gravestone was heartfelt: OUR PRECIOUS ONE FROM US HAS GONE. A VOICE WE LOVED HAS STILLED, A PLACE IS VACANT IN OUR HOME, WHICH NEVER CAN BE FILLED. Photo by the author.

son-in-law and the senior member of the family's next generation, was the logical candidate to lead the vengeance-seekers. The former lawman was an experienced gunhand, and he took the fight to his family's adversaries.

Harrison Hamer, on some sort of business, traveled to Post City and checked into the Algerita Hotel, where Gee McMeans and Gladys Johnson Sims had faced off with drawn pistols in the upstairs hallway in July 1916. Harrison left his guns in his room, but in the lobby downstairs he was provoked by Gee McMeans, who was armed with a brace of revolvers. The unarmed Hamer wisely refused to let himself be goaded into a fight, and McMeans sauntered off with an arrogant laugh.

An eyewitness telephoned Frank Hamer about the dangerous encounter. Frank announced "that if anyone murdered my brother that they would pay dearly for it and immediately thereafter the hatred of the entire bunch was directed toward me." Frank further claimed that "McMeans openly boasted the fact that he would kill me on sight, as witnesses from Fort Worth to El Paso testified. I did not know McMeans."[4] But soon enough Hamer would meet McMeans face to face.

On a morning in September 1917, when Frank and Harrison were accompanying Billy Johnson on the drive into Snyder, the party spotted a big gray wolf. The car halted, Frank stepped out with a rifle, then began firing at the predator on a distant horizon. Four armed men suddenly jumped up from a point of concealment near the line of fire. An ambush had been set beside the ranch road, but the gunmen apparently thought that somehow they had been discovered. Believing they were under fire from the deadly Frank Hamer, the would-be assassins ran to their car and sped away toward Snyder.

In town Frank and Harrison recognized two of the bushwhackers lurking beside the First National Bank. The Hamer brothers cuffed both men around. "I grabbed him by the collar and shoved him up against the abutment of the First National Bank building," recalled Harrison, "and smashed his nose and his lips and all." Frank offered a challenge to fight with pistols, then the men were permitted to depart.[5]

This incident may have happened late in September 1917, following the trial of Gladys Hamer. Insisting that he needed Gladys as a witness for Sidney Johnson, Cullen Higgins succeeded in having her charges reduced from murder to assault with intent to kill. Her case was brought to court in Lamesa on Monday, September 17, 1917. The trial packet is missing from the courthouse in Lamesa, but volume 1 of the *Criminal File Docket* and volume 1 of the *District Court Criminal Minutes* reveal that Cullen Higgins persuaded the district attorney to drop charges against Gladys.[6] Although the record of Cullen's legal arguments is unavailable, it had to be persuasive that Gladys was the sole surviving parent of the two little girls (whose new stepfather was the highly regarded Frank Hamer); that the bullets she fired did not produce the fatal wounds; and that she was a female in 1916 Texas.

It is unfortunate that the arguments of Cullen Higgins no longer exist and that his expertise in this difficult case may not be studied. But the missing testimony is part of an extralegal pattern, a pattern that may well have involved Judge Higgins. When the author first researched the Johnson-Sims Feud during the late 1990s, the trial envelopes at the courthouses in Snyder, Lamesa, and Baird were virtually empty. Except for a few subpoenas and other minor documents, each trial packet was devoid of court testimony. It seems likely that Billy Johnson had the testimony against Gladys and Sidney removed and destroyed. Reputedly Johnson once arranged a cover-up of a shooting by young Gladys against two men who accosted her. Now the prominent rancher-banker evidently erased the legal record against his children in the shooting death of Ed Sims. If Johnson was responsible for the disappearance of the trial testimony, it is probable that he dispatched his longtime attorney on this mission. Judge Higgins, of course, was familiar with all three courthouses and with most of the county officials. It would have been easy for Judge Higgins to gain access to the trial packets on cases he recently had represented. In each of the rural West Texas courthouses, Judge Higgins could have removed the testimony and replaced the trial envelopes with no suspicion. Admittedly, Cullen Higgins was respected as a deeply religious man and an ethical representative of the law; some other attorney could have been dispatched to the courthouses. But no one other than Billy Johnson had a motive to tamper with these particular trial documents, while Cullen Higgins would have been the logical—if not the only—candidate to send to the courthouses.

Cullen Higgins made it possible for Gladys to appear in court in Baird two weeks after her trial. On Monday, October 1, 1917, Gladys entered the Callahan County courthouse, along with her husband, his brother Harrison, her brother Emmett, and dozens of other witnesses subpoenaed to "personally appear" at Sidney Johnson's trial. Among others called were Billy Johnson, Gladys's daughters, Emmett's wife, and Bill Wren, along with Gee McMeans, Bob Higgins, and Si Bostick. A special venire of forty-eight potential jurors also assembled. But the day's proceedings quickly ended, "continued by agreement" until the spring term.[7]

Dozens of people summoned to Baird now, abruptly and unexpectedly, headed for home. Gladys's daughters apparently returned to Snyder with their grandfather and aunt, perhaps by train. Frank, Gladys, Harrison, and Emmett piled into an automobile to drive back to Snyder. Frank Hamer received a tip that Gee McMeans and other gunmen were planning an attack. A southpaw, Frank had his .45—nicknamed "Old Lucky"—strapped on his left hip. As a backup, he belted on another handgun, a Smith and Wesson .44.

The party drove through Abilene, then proceeded to Sweetwater, fifty miles to the west. About half past one Hamer drove by Sweetwater's tall Bluebonnet Hotel, then pulled into a garage on the southeast corner of the square to have a punctured tire repaired. Gladys stayed in the auto while Harrison and Emmett went in search of a toilet and Frank walked to the office.

Among the astounded citizens who saw the impending shootout were members of a Nolan County grand jury. With a new courthouse

The Bluebonnet Hotel stood half a block east of the square in Sweetwater. On October 1, 1917, a grand jury was meeting in the hotel because the new courthouse (seen with white columns left of center) was still under construction. When a gun battle broke out at the southeast corner of the square (left edge of photo at center), grand jury members looked out to view the action. Courtesy Pioneer Museum, Sweetwater.

under construction on Sweetwater's town square, the county had rented rooms for official purposes in the Bluebonnet Hotel. The hotel overlooked the scene of the shootout, and a grand jury was meeting in one of the rooms. When jury members heard gunfire, they scurried to the windows and became eyewitnesses.

Within moments after Hamer stopped at the garage, another car drove up, and Gee McMeans and H. E. Phillips descended. Perhaps McMeans had sped to Sweetwater to intercept Hamer, or perhaps he had followed closely, looking for an opportunity to corner his prey. Perhaps the ensuing gun battle was pre-planned, or perhaps it was spontaneous.

When Frank Hamer emerged from the garage office he encountered Gee McMeans, who leveled a .45 automatic. McMeans fired at pointblank range, and the heavy slug slammed into Hamer's left shoulder. McMeans had shot the famous Frank Hamer, and he was triumphant: "I've got you now, God damn you!"[8]

But Hamer reacted instantly, swiping with his right hand at the .45 automatic. The gun was knocked downward just as McMeans again pulled the trigger, and the second bullet tore into Hamer's right thigh. Then the automatic jammed and Hamer, ignoring his wounds, went on the attack. The wounded Ranger seized the barrel of the automatic, wrenched it from the grasp of McMeans, then began pounding his assailant with his right fist.

While Hamer fought for his life against McMeans, H. E. Phillips crossed the street clutching a shotgun. Still seated in the car, Gladys spotted the gunman advancing on her husband from behind. She pulled up her automatic, screamed out a warning to Frank, and opened fire. When bullets began to strike near him from an unexpected direction, Phillips ducked behind a parked car. He tried to advance again, but once more Gladys drove him back to cover. When Phillips swung his shotgun toward Gladys, she continued shooting and again sent him ducking for safety.

At last Gladys emptied her clip, and Phillips dashed over to the two men grappling in front of the garage. McMeans twisted free from

Hamer just as Phillips triggered a shotgun blast at the head of the tall lawman. Buckshot ripped away Hamer's hat brim.

"I got him! I got him!" exclaimed Phillips. Hamer sank to his knees, shaking his head from the ear-splitting report of the shotgun. But the buckshot had only wounded his hat, and Hamer struggled to his feet, drawing his Smith and Wesson with his right hand. Hamer's two assailants hastily retreated to their car, where McMeans rearmed himself with a pump shotgun. But Hamer, close behind, leveled his .44 and drilled McMeans through the heart. Gee McMeans dropped dead on the sidewalk. Phillips "hunkered down beside the dead man" and lost all desire to battle Frank Hamer.[9]

"I invited him to get up and fight me face to face," related Hamer years later, "but he immediately broke and ran down the sidewalk with his shotgun in his hand—I called for him to turn around, not caring to shoot him in the back."[10]

Harrison Hamer had no such compunctions. Hearing gunshots from inside the toilet, Harrison barreled out to the car and seized a Winchester. He sprinted over to his brother and leveled his rifle at the retreating Phillips. Frank reached out and thrust the Winchester barrel upward just as Harrison fired. Hearing the shot, Phillips bolted through the side door of a cafe as Harrison gave chase. Although Harrison came back empty-handed, within a short time Phillips was arrested by a Sweetwater policeman.

Following a fatal shooting in the Old West, it was customary to assemble a coroner's jury immediately. If the victim was armed, the jury almost always ruled that the shooting was self-defense, which closed the legal proceedings almost before the gunsmoke had cleared.

Nearly two decades into the twentieth century, West Texans remained connected in spirit, custom, and outlook to the Old West. The Nolan County grand jury members invited Frank Hamer, a tough peace officer who commanded respect and admiration, to join them for a prompt legal closure to the gun battle. While a doctor began working on Hamer's wounds, the grand jury stated that they had witnessed the encounter and that Hamer shot McMeans in self-defense.

Commending the wounded officer for resisting the temptation to shoot Phillips in the back, the grand jury no-billed Hamer. With legalities now completed, Hamer retired to submit to more thorough medical treatment.

Frank Hamer had been shot twice with a .45. When he was able to travel, Frank journeyed to California, accompanied by Gladys, Trix, and Beverly. Their destination was a house in the Los Angeles area which Billy Johnson had purchased as a summer home. The family stayed for several months while Frank recuperated fully. Everyone enjoyed the California climate and a leisurely vacation. Gladys was pregnant, and Frank Hamer Jr. was born on April 11, 1918.[11]

During their extended stay in California, the family toured Universal Studios. Then, as now, Universal earned extra income by permitting curious tourists an inside look at the making of motion pictures. While in Hollywood, Frank Hamer was introduced to a rising star of silent Westerns, Tom Mix. Western movies were a staple of the film industry, and Mix would reach superstar status by the 1920s. Publicity boasts about Mix included his involvement in the Boer War, the Boxer Rebellion, the Philippine Insurrection, and the Mexican Revolution, as well as his service as a U.S. marshal and as a Texas Ranger. Although Mix had done none of these things, he had enlisted in the U.S. Army as a young man and, among other adventures, worked in rodeos and Wild West shows. In 1910 he began making short films. A superb rider with a strong physique and rugged good looks, Mix was a natural as a cowboy or lawman of the silver screen.

Mix was deeply impressed when he met a real lawman, Texas Ranger Frank Hamer, who was recovering from wounds after killing his most recent attacker. Frank Hamer was the embodiment of the stalwart characters Tom Mix played onscreen: fearless, an expert gunman, a product of the Old West. Mix befriended Hamer, taking him to the sets of various films in progress, and talking to him about trying his hand in the movies. They were photographed together, and the Texas Ranger was taller than the movie star. Although the world of cinematic make-believe held no appeal for Hamer, Mix later visited Frank in Texas.

The Hamers at last piled into an automobile for the scenic drive back to Snyder. During the lengthy absence of Frank and Gladys from West Texas, the final and most tragic violence of the Johnson-Sims Feud erupted in Clairemont and Sweetwater.

The California home of Billy and Nannie Johnson in the Los Angeles area. Billy and Nannie spent long periods here, and Frank and Gladys Hamer, along with their children, came here after the Sweetwater shootout. Courtesy Betty M. Giddens.

Chapter 9

Assassination and Retribution

"JUDGE CULLEN C. HIGGINS MURDERED SUN-DAY NIGHT"

Snyder Signal, March 22, 1918

Ada Sims McMeans took the remains of her husband back to Odessa for burial. The oldest daughter of Dave and Laura Belle Sims now was a widow, her husband killed in a shootout with Frank Hamer—who was married to Gladys Sims Hamer. The oldest son of Dave and Laura Belle earlier had been shot to death by Gladys and her brother Sidney. The losses of the Sims family were staggering.

But while the family tried to cope with their latest loss, Gladys was vacationing in California and Sidney, out on bail, returned to his wife, Ruth, and three-year-old son, Weldon. Gladys was free from all charges in the death of Ed Sims, thanks to the legal skills of Judge Cullen Higgins. Judge Higgins had represented Gladys in her bitter divorce from Ed Sims and in custody arrangements for Trix and Beverly. Currently Judge Higgins was acting as a special prosecutor, preparing a murder case for the pending trial of Will Luman, who was free on bail. Soon Judge Higgins would represent Sidney Johnson in Baird, when the district court again would take up the homicide of Ed Sims. With his recent string of successes and obvious ability as an attorney, it seemed likely that Judge Higgins once more would work his legal magic and win acquittal for Sidney. For the Sims family, it was bad enough that Gladys Sims had gone free, but the prospect of exoneration for the shotgun-wielding Sidney was almost too much to bear.

With astounding audacity, a decision was made to target Judge Higgins for assassination. The team of assassins who would stalk the judge was Will Luman, Si Bostick, and Bob Higdon. Luman, of course, could be expected to resent Special Prosecutor Higgins. And Luman was an expert gunman with little reservation about resorting to violence. Si Bostick, a cattle thief and lowlife, was willing to join an assassination team that included Will Luman, who had killed his father the previous year. Bob Higdon was thought to have been a tardy member of the attack team which unsuccessfully battled Frank Hamer in Sweetwater.

Was this trio paid, or promised pay, to assassinate Judge Cullen Higgins? Although no proof exists, it seems inconceivable that three gunmen would risk the certain fury of the law without the incentive of monetary reward. The likelihood that Dave Sims provided money to avenge the death of his son is underscored by the fact that Sims later stood Higdon's bond on the charge of murder.[1] Whatever their motivation, Luman, Bostick, and Higdon armed themselves and hunted Cullen Higgins.

A leading citizen of Snyder, Cullen was active in the Methodist Church and the Masonic Lodge. In 1916 he moved his wife and son into a new brick house. In his early forties, Cullen Higgins was handsome, popular, successful, and widely admired as a pillar of the law in West Texas. He never suspected that by March 1918 he was being stalked by a team of hired assassins.

Judge Higgins was involved in several cases scheduled to be heard in a district court session at Clairemont, beginning on Monday, March 18, 1918. Sunday, March 17, was filled with church activities. On Sunday morning in Snyder, Higgins taught his boys' Sunday School class at the Methodist Church, then attended worship services. After lunch at home, Higgins bade farewell to his wife and little boy before setting out for Clairemont, thirty-five miles to the northeast. The only church at Clairemont was holding a revival, and the devout Higgins participated in evening services.

Judge Cullen Higgins, the most tragic victim of the Johnson-Sims Feud. Courtesy Samantha Usnick.

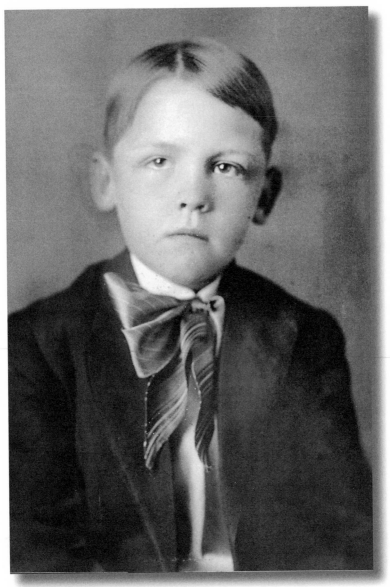

Marshall Cullen Higgins, only child of Cullen and Olive. Marshall spent his entire career as a law enforcement officer. Courtesy Samantha Usnick.

Cullen Higgins built this home for his family in 1917, but he would live in it only a short time before he was murdered. Photo by Karon O'Neal.

After church Cullen spoke words of encouragement to a few young men who had been converted, then strolled to Clairemont's two-story frame hotel. In the lobby he encountered his successor as district judge, John B. Thomas, and a court reporter named Wiess. While these men talked, Si Bostick, Bob Higdon, and Will Luman crept up to a window overlooking the hotel lobby.

Cullen Higgins sat with his back to the window. One of the assassins aimed a shotgun and triggered a load of buckshot, blasting Cullen out of his chair. "Confusion reigned" in the hotel lobby, while the gunmen fled into the darkness, mounted their waiting horses, then galloped west out of town. The stricken Cullen Higgins was carried to his room, where "friends did what they could." A telephone call to Snyder summoned Olive Higgins, and she was brought to her husband's bedside by numerous friends.[2]

Soon it was decided to seek medical help at "a sanitarium" in Spur, about twenty miles to the north. At Spur on Monday a physician extracted five buckshot, but probing instruments could not locate two of the slugs. Early in the afternoon internal surgery revealed that Cullen's intestines had been perforated, and his wife and friends feared the worst. On Tuesday Cullen began failing, although he remained conscious. He calmly told those at his bedside that he was ready to go, and he died at twenty minutes past noon. Only forty-two, Cullen Higgins had survived his gunfighting father by merely three and a half years.

Members of the Masonic Lodge formed a procession to escort the remains of their fraternal brother twenty miles toward Snyder, where a procession of Snyder Masons brought the body to the new Higgins home. Tom Higgins came by train from Lampasas, packing a revolver in case he had to defend himself. Although West Texas was sparsely settled, a crowd estimated at two thousand assembled in Snyder, including friends from New Mexico, Oklahoma, and Colorado. The funeral was held on Wednesday afternoon. Religious services were conducted by two ministers at the Methodist Church, followed by the Masonic funeral ritual at the Snyder Cemetery north of town. Perhaps

The courthouse in Clairemont in its original form. The man at upper right is perched on the second-floor porch of the hotel, northeast of the courthouse, where Cullen Higgins was assassinated. Courtesy Betty M. Giddens.

two hundred Masons were among the graveside crowd to honor their fallen brother.

"The people of Snyder and Scurry County are bound together in deep grief this week," reported the *Snyder Signal* two days after the funeral. "And overwhelmed in sorrow because of the enactment of a cruel tragedy seldom equaled in atrocity, one which touches the heart and life of the entire community and casts a dark pall of gloom over a happy home."[3]

Later in the article the *Signal* posed a burning question: "Why was he murdered? We don't know." Area lawmen wasted little time in finding answers. Court Reporter Wiess told Kent County Sheriff R. I. Goodall that shortly before the shooting he had noticed Si Bostick on the porch of the hotel. Sheriff Goodall telephoned the sheriff's office at Post City, where Bostick now resided with his wife and children. Texas Rangers Sam McKenzie and H. L. Koons, stationed in Sweetwater, were dispatched to Post City to arrest Bostick.

To no one's surprise, Bostick was not at home. But McKenzie and Koons initiated a search of the countryside, soon locating the fugitive at the ranch of Tom Askins, about twelve miles north of Post City. The Rangers arrested Bostick on Tuesday at midday—during the very hour that Cullen Higgins died.

Bostick was jailed at Post City, but feelings ran so high that there was fear of a lynching. On Wednesday, Rangers McKenzie and Koons spirited their prisoner to an unknown location, then unobtrusively brought him aboard a train, perhaps in the baggage car. Late Wednesday night the trio arrived by rail in Sweetwater, and the Rangers hustled Bostick into a third-floor cell at the red brick jail on the northeast corner of the courthouse square. Bostick was the only prisoner on the third floor, and because of the secretive late arrival, no one—except law officers—knew the suspected assassin was in town.

During this era of law enforcement, harsh interrogation methods were used to extract information from prisoners. Not long after being confined in his lonely cell, Bostick revealed the names of his accomplices, Bob Higdon and Will Luman. Alerts went out to lawmen in

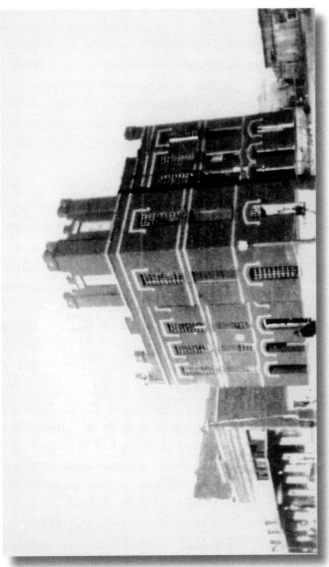

The old Nolan County Jail stood on the northeast corner of the square in Sweetwater. Confined here after his arrest as a suspect in the murder of Cullen Higgins, Si Bostick was found dead in his cell. Courtesy Pioneer Museum, Sweetwater.

likely locations, and on Thursday Higdon and Luman were arrested in Post City. They were taken to Snyder and incarcerated under heavy guard.

In the Sweetwater jail, Bostick had told officers the identity of his fellow gunmen, the location of the murder weapon, and apparently everything else he was asked. There was little more for him to reveal, and seething fury was directed against this murderer of a prominent member of the region's law enforcement community. On Friday morning, March 22, Deputy Sheriff T. B. Thompson arrived at Bostick's cell with breakfast. But the prisoner did not answer Thompson's greeting, and a moment later the deputy scurried downstairs to summon Sheriff T. B. Thompson.

Within a short time Sheriff Thompson, the county health officer, and other officials were crowding into the cell to examine the prisoner's lifeless body. Bostick's belt was tightened around his neck and connected by a torn strip of bedsheet to a bar on the window. A pocket handkerchief was stuffed into his mouth. Bostick had been dead for several hours, but his neck was not broken, and he was leaning against the wall—with his bare feet touching the floor.

"HANGS SELF IN CELL," headlined the *Sweetwater Daily Republic* the following day. The newspaper speculated that Bostick had pulled "the strap around his neck taut enough to induce death by choking." An inquest conducted by Justice of the Peace John Bryan ruled that the prisoner's death "was self-committed by hanging."[4]

It is impossible to believe that a man with his feet on the floor would lean hard enough and long enough against a belt noose to kill himself by slow strangulation. Supposedly, too, Bostick was considerate enough to stuff a handkerchief in his mouth to muffle any outcry, especially since no other prisoners were on the third floor.

Although it strains credulity that Si Bostick killed himself in such an excruciating—and improbable—manner, no lynch mob was involved. Bostick had been delivered to Sweetwater in secret, and the public was unaware of his presence in town. But peace officers knew where Bostick was held, and rumors began circulating that lawmen had slipped into his cell. Certainly it would not have been unusual in 1918 for officers to conduct a heavy-handed interrogation in a lonely cell. And if an accused murderer later was discovered hanged, other officials might readily suggest suicide in order to protect members of the law enforcement fraternity who provided a rough measure of justice. No official documents exist about Si Bostick's hanging, only a newspaper account which describes a dubious "suicide." Higgins descendants continue to believe—approvingly—that lawmen killed Bostick.

The most plausible advocates of this story were brothers Frank and Nath (short for Nathan) Terry, who were first cousins of Cullen Higgins. Frank and Nath were sons of Malinda Higgins Terry, who was Pink's sister and Cullen's aunt. Frank and Nath were lawmen, and both were future sheriffs of Fisher County. Furious over the cold-blooded murder of their cousin, Frank and Nath joined a posse which rode in search of the murder weapon on the day after Bostick's hanging. Bostick owned the shotgun, but he had insisted that Bob Higdon pulled the trigger in Clairemont.

Obviously Bostick confessed where the shotgun was discarded after the killers fled the shooting site. The posse rode to a stock tank between Clairemont and Post City. Nath Terry stripped off his clothes and dove into the frigid water, soon emerging with the shotgun. A reasonable assumption could be that Si Bostick told about the shotgun and anything else they wanted to know to nocturnal visitors who were threatening to hang him.[5]

After Si Bostick died in his cell, Bob Higdon and Will Luman were transferred from Snyder to the jail in Anson, then driven by the sheriff and a deputy to more secure confinement in Fort Worth. Indictments for the murder of Cullen Higgins were handed down against Higdon and Luman. Although Higdon was thought to have fired the fatal blast, the deceased Si Bostick became the sacrificial lamb for justice. The identical indictments charged that Higdon (and Luman) did "advise, command and encourage the said Si Bostick to do and

Nath Terry and his wife, Jessie. Nath found the shotgun used in the murder of Cullen Higgins, and later he became sheriff of Fisher County. Courtesy Bob Terry.

commit the said murder, the said R. N. Higdon [and Will Luman] not being personally present when said offense was committed by the said Si Bostick."[6]

Once it was legally stated that Higdon and Luman were not present when Cullen Higgins was murdered, then it was "agreed by the attorneys representing the state that the case is a bailable one." Bail was set at $10,000 for each defendant. Four friends combined to post $10,000 for the release of Will Luman, while Dave Sims was one of two men who pledged "their land, tenements, [and] goods chattles [sic]" for Bob Higdon's bond. The general view was that Higdon had fired the fatal blast into Cullen Higgins, and that he had been hired by Sims to avenge the death of his son, while Luman came along because of his own resentment of Special Prosecutor Higgins.[7]

At the September 1918 term of district court in Clairemont, Judge John B. Thomas ruled that the trials of Higdon and Luman should be moved from Clairemont, the site of the assassination, to Haskell for the November district court term. Although these trials were postponed, in 1919 Luman was convicted of manslaughter in the death of Joshua Bostick. He was sentenced to five years in prison, and he would earn early release. Higdon never stood trial for the killing of Joshua Bostick, and after various legal delays neither Higdon nor Luman was tried for the murder of Cullen Higgins. Higdon and Luman were the beneficiaries of the death, while in custody, of their hard-luck confederate, Si Bostick.[8]

Deciding that he no longer would push his luck as a hired killer, Bob Higdon permanently assumed a low profile. Will Luman returned to Post City. He was married three times, and when he caught his second wife with an extramarital sweetheart, he shot them both. Acquitted by a sympathetic jury, Will married his former wife's sister, who raised her two niece-stepdaughters. Will's son by his first marriage, Pud, was a great athlete at Post High School, starring on Antelope football teams during the mid-1920s.[9]

Capitalizing on Luman's notoriety as a hard case, the Texas and Southwestern Cattle Raisers Association hired Will as an undercover

man. Luman proved to be an ideal field agent, and later he was pro-
moted to inspector. Moving to Borger, Luman worked for the association for nearly three decades. He died at the age of eighty-six in 1977,
having earned wide respect for his long career in law enforcement.[10]

Two weeks after the shooting of Cullen Higgins, on Monday, April
1, 1918, Sidney Johnson reappeared in court at Baird. Until his recent
death, Cullen Higgins had been Sidney's lead attorney, and the new
counsel needed time to prepare a defense. The judge again granted a
continuance, to September 23, 1918. The audacious murder of Sidney
Johnson's attorney brought even greater attention than before to his
trial. Judge Joe Burkett opened proceedings on Monday, September
23, and a jury was selected from a special venire of seventy-two men.
Although the testimony has vanished from the documents in the trial
packet, within two days the jury returned a verdict of not guilty.[11]

The Sims family must have been anguished by a sense of injustice.
Sidney Johnson was free. No legal consequences had been suffered by
the men who blasted Ed Sims as he lay on a street, wounded by Gladys
Johnson Sims—who also went free. No one paid a legal price for the
murder of Ed Sims.

Extralegal attempts to extract a measure of justice had resulted in
the deaths of Gee McMeans and Cullen Higgins. But there would be no
further efforts to impose extralegal justice through gunplay. The rapid
arrests of the three assassins of Cullen Higgins and the subsequent
death of Si Bostick in his jail cell, emphatically delivered the message
that further gunplay by Johnson or Sims partisans would not be toler-
ated. Area gunmen should beware: any additional violence connected
to the feud might well prove "suicidal."

Another discouragement to further feud malevolence was the loss
of both family patriarchs. Years of disreputable behavior by his family and of violent events shattered Billy Johnson. He had worked his
way to a position of power and wealth and prominence, only to see his
family's reputation sullied by the sordid infidelity of Gladys, by her
nasty divorce, by the murder of his former son-in-law in front of his
bank—a murder executed by his son and daughter and witnessed by

Dave Sims died less than thee years after his oldest son, and was buried beside him. Laura Belle lived to the age of ninety-one. Photo by the author.

his little granddaughters. Later a wild shootout in Sweetwater again involved his daughter and resulted in the wounding of his new son-in-law. Then his friend and attorney, the estimable Cullen Higgins, was brutally slain in another shotgun attack. The widow of Ed Sims initiated legal action in district court at Snyder: "Mrs. Mildred Sims vs. W. A. Johnson, et al., suit for damages."[12] Billy was staggered by blow after blow to his sense of respectability and integrity. "Tragedy came to the Johnson family," summed up a friend.[13] After years of intense stress Billy Johnson cracked. He suffered a nervous breakdown, and he would never be the same, mentally or physically. Billy and Nannie left the ranch and moved to California, remaining away from West Texas for several years. Sidney moved into the big ranch house.

Several months after the acquittal of Sidney Johnson, sixty-one-year old Dave Sims succumbed to some form of cancer. Confined to his bed in the sturdy ranch house he had built, Sims died on Friday, May 23, 1919.[14] Three days after he died, Dave Sims was buried beside his oldest son in the cemetery at Post City. The Johnson-Sims Feud was at an end, although hard feelings would persist.

Chapter 10

Aftermath and Redemption

"I sometimes think of the long ago as the most harrowing terrible dream imaginable...."

Rocky Higgins Johnson

An important element of classic tragedy is redemption. In *Romeo and Juliet* the Capulets and Montagues reconciled over the corpses of the young lovers. But there would be no Johnson-Sims reconciliation in West Texas.

Kelly Sims remained so unreconciled to the murder of his older brother, Ed, that he refused ever to set foot in Snyder. Kelly was certain that if he ever sighted Sidney Johnson that he would kill him. Although his wife could not be deterred from occasional trips into Snyder for shopping, Kelly insisted that she carry a gun in her purse. Kelly always packed a pistol, a .45 automatic that was the deadliest handgun of the time. At night the .45 always went beneath his pillow, and before going to bed Kelly propped an automatic shotgun beside the bedroom window. Many years later Kelly refused an opportunity to buy a four-section parcel of land because it belonged to Weldon Johnson, Sidney's son. Laura Belle Sims remained so bitter over the death of her oldest son that she found it hard to accept the overtures of Trix Johnson McMullan, her granddaughter. Trix was the daughter

A lifelong rancher, Kelly Sims named his son after his murdered older brother. Courtesy Ed and Anne Sims.

Automatic pistol carried as a precaution by Sweet Sims—especially when she went shopping in Snyder. Her son, Ed, now owns the gun. Photo by the author.

of Gladys, and Laura Belle could barely bring herself to be civil to Trix or to her little son and daughter—Laura Belle's great-grandchildren.[1]

If redemption would not be achieved through reconciliation between the Johnson and Sims clans, individual family members could—and did—restore honor to their families. Numerous Johnson and Sims descendants continued the ranching traditions that had brought prosperity and identity to their families. And each family produced an individual who achieved widespread recognition of a positive nature. Frank Hamer, a Sims son-in-law, became celebrated through his law enforcement exploits.

When the Hamer family—Frank, Gladys, baby Frank Jr., and Trix and Beverly Sims—returned to Scurry County from California in 1918, the violence of the Johnson-Sims Feud had ceased. Although Frank's bullet wounds were healed, the deeper wounds of loss and blame and hatred remained raw among members of both families.

Frank Hamer re-enlisted in the Texas Rangers on October 1, 1918, and four days later he engaged in a wild shootout against liquor smugglers along the Rio Grande near Brownsville. Sgt. Delbert Timberlake of Company C was one of the casualties, and Hamer was elevated to the sergeant's vacancy. For a year and a half during 1920 and 1921 he served the United States Prohibition Service, before rejoining the Rangers as captain of Company C. "There is not a criminal in Texas who does not fear and respect him," asserted Walter P. Webb.[2]

While Hamer battled smugglers in South Texas, Gladys and her children made their home at the big Johnson ranch house. Trix and Beverly had attended school in California, and now were in elementary school in Snyder. Frank visited his family at the Johnson ranch whenever possible, and in 1921 Gladys gave birth to Billy Hamer.

Nannie, as critical as ever, was openly abrasive toward her son-in-law, and Frank Hamer responded to her in kind. During one of their squabbles, Nannie became angry. "Oh, I wish I were a man for one minute," she snapped. "Believe me, Madam," said Hamer meaningfully, "so do I."[3]

In 1922 Frank Hamer was made captain of the Ranger Headquarters Company in Austin. Captain Hamer bought a house on Riverside Drive. Putting his saddle, boots, and spurs in storage, he wore business suits and ties and shoes. But Hamer always carried Old Lucky, the single-action colt .45 that was a dependable throwback to the nineteenth century.

Gladys and the children moved to Austin. Trix and Beverly enrolled in Austin High School, a large brick facility just west of downtown. Any time they went out after dark, Hamer insisted that they carry guns. Trix and Beverly kept their pistols in the glove compartment, while Gladys, of course, was never without her automatic. Indeed, the events of 1916 and 1917 had done nothing to render Gladys reluctant to use her gun, as she would prove in later years.

At the age of sixteen Beverly journeyed on the Southern Pacific Railroad for a visit to her grandparents in California. When the westbound train stopped in San Antonio, one of the passengers who boarded was movie star Richard Arlen. Arlen was in San Antonio, along with Clara Bow, Buddy Rogers, and a large cast and crew, to film *Wings*, which would become the first movie to win the Academy Award for Best Motion Picture. The classic was lensed primarily at Randolph Field, San Antonio's "West Point of the Air." Arlen was making a quick visit to his fiancée, actress Geneva Ralston, but he invited the beautiful young Texas lady to eat with him in the dining car.[4]

Billy and Nannie Johnson spent an extended time in California, hoping that the climate and physicians might restore his health. His nerves were shattered, he suffered from a skin condition, and while stepping out of his shower he tripped and broke a hip, which confined him to a wheelchair. But the family reunited at the ranch each summer. Frank Jr., raised in Austin, fondly remembered his summers at the ranch.[5]

On one occasion in West Texas, Trix and Beverly traveled over to Post City with the intention of suing the executors of their father's estate. Their uncle, Kelly Sims, was the principal executor, but no lawsuit developed. Perhaps Kelly responded to the threat of legal action, or perhaps he simply decided to do the right thing by his brother's daughters. In his last will, Ed Sims bitterly changed the beneficiaries of a $20,000 life insurance policy from Trix and Beverly to Kelly, who seems to have returned the $20,000 to his nieces.[6]

When each girl turned eighteen, she received an "inheritance" of $10,000. On the day in 1927 when Beverly was given her $10,000 check, she purchased a blue roadster with a jump seat. Beverly and Trix drove to California in the new car. When they were ready to return, their grandmother came with them, riding in the jump seat. After Billy and Nannie moved back to West Texas, Nannie bought an automobile and learned to drive.[7]

Trix also moved back to West Texas, embracing the ranching heritage she absorbed from both sides of her family. Trix was a horsewoman who loved ranch life, and she married a rancher. Vern McMullan, more than a decade older than Trix, was one of nine children raised on a ranch adjacent to the Johnson spread. The McMullan ranch, just south of the Johnson property, consisted of six or seven sections. The Johnsons and McMullans were neighbors, and after Trix and Vern married, Billy and Nannie gave them half a section of land across the road from the McMullan place. Trix also owned four sections from the Garza County ranch of her mother and father. Beverly wanted no part of ranch life. She married Vern's brother, Rudy McMullan, and had a son. But Beverly soon divorced Rudy, then married an architect, Albert Benson (who designed the tower on the University of Texas campus), and had another son. The Bensons lived in other states, and Trix acquired Beverly's interest in the Garza County property.[8]

Trix and Vern built a single-story brick house on their Johnson half-section. The front porch spanned the entire width of the house. There were two bedrooms, a cellar, and a large living room featuring an ornate fireplace. Trix and Vern had a son and a daughter, Billy Bob and Ann. Born in 1926, Billy Bob was five years younger than Billy Hamer, but the uncle and nephew became close playmates.

As a young lady during the 1920s, Helen Trix
Sims was dressed and coiffed in the latest flapper
style. But ranching was in her blood, and soon
Trix moved from Austin to Scurry County,
spending the rest of her life as a rancher. Courtesy
Billy Bob McMullan.

Beverly Sims became a beautiful and stylish young woman. At ninety-nine she remains vivacious and humorous with a keen memory. Courtesy Beverly Sims.

Trix once took her children to see their Sims grandmother at Laura Belle's Kent County ranch house. But Laura Belle was unpleasant, and when they were driving away. Billy Bob said, "Mama, I don't want to go back." Billy Bob did not go back, even though Trix returned with his little sister, Ann. Trix reached out to her grandmother Sims, trying to reconnect with her father's family. But Laura Belle, who had lost her oldest son, husband, and oldest son-in-law within a traumatic two-and-one-half year period, remained distant.[9]

Laura Belle survived her husband by thirty-seven years. She stayed on the home ranch, which was managed by her son, John Tom "Red" Sims. The original Sims brand was an OXO, and Red used an OTO, while his sister Sallie branded OSO. Under Red's management the Sims ranch became noted for its fine horses, and Sims mares were in wide demand. In advanced age Laura Belle reluctantly agreed to move to a house in Post, where she died in 1956 at ninety-one. Her oldest daughter, Ada, died a few months later at fifty-one. Following the death of her husband at the hands of Frank Hamer, Ada McMeans moved with her little boy, Walter, to New Mexico—the original destination of her parents in 1888, when she was five. Ada Sims McMeans died in Fort Sumner, the final haunt of Billy the Kid.[10]

It may have been of some satisfaction to Laura Belle Sims and Ada McMeans that they survived Frank Hamer, who died in 1955 at the age of seventy-one. But by the time of his death, Captain Hamer had been famous for more then two decades as the man who tracked down the iconic Depression outlaws, Clyde Barrow and Bonnie Parker. In 1934, with the Texas couple on a crime spree of robbery and murder, Captain Hamer was asked to lead a manhunt by Marshal Lee Simmons, head of the state prison system. Bonnie and Clyde had engineered a bloody prison break, springing five prisoners with a murderous fusillade. Simmons created the position of Special Investigator for the Texas Prison System and persuaded Hamer, who had gone on inactive status with the Rangers in 1932, to accept the assignment. Assisted by other officers, Hamer trapped Bonnie and Clyde on May 23, 1934, near Gibsland, Louisiana. The outlaw couple died in a torrent of gunfire.

Newspaper headlines across the country focused attention on Frank Hamer, and he was the subject of special resolutions from the U.S. Congress and the Texas Legislature. Already well-known and greatly respected within the law enforcement profession, Captain Hamer suddenly had a national reputation. He received thousands of congratulatory telegrams and letters, including one from longtime admirer Tom Mix. He turned down a series of offers to tell his story on film or the printed page. Seventeen years after he traded bullets with Gee McMeans in Sweetwater, Frank Hamer became renowned for the greatest exploit of a long career spent in imposing law and order.[11]

Billy Johnson, beset by health problems, was rocked by another blow in 1927. In California Billy and Nannie received word that Emmett, their oldest son, had died under mysterious circumstances. Two years earlier Emmett suffered a nervous breakdown. Seeking a more favorable climate, Emmett, Rocky, and their two children moved to the Wichita Falls area. The Johnson ranch land that Emmett had worked for nearly two decades reverted to original ownership when he moved, and his heirs would have no claim to the property that had been their home since the marriage of Rocky and Emmett in 1907. On their twentieth anniversary, May 5, 1927, Emmett "accidentally shot himself to death" at his home near Wichita Falls. While Emmett and another man were working on a roadside fence, a boy on a runaway horse triggered a sudden scramble. Emmett's rifle, propped against a fence, toppled over and discharged. Emmett "was instantly paralyzed," according to the mortician. "They said a smile just broke over his face and he didn't say anything," wrote his nineteen-year-old daughter, "Dugie," to her grandmother in California. Emmett was only forty-one.[12]

Emmett's corpse was shipped to Snyder for burial. Billy and Nannie could not come for the funeral, but everyone in Snyder remembered that Emmett had "a princely heart, was of a cheerful and happy disposition, kind and considerate always." Following Emmett's funeral at the Methodist Church, "a great concourse of friends followed him to his resting place" at the Snyder Cemetery.[13] With a scant inheritance, the widowed Rocky soon ventured to the booming Rio Grande Valley. She farmed and sold real estate. Through the years Rocky wrote long, revealing letters to her daughter, Dugie, who married L. W. "Dusty" Miller in 1929. This invaluable correspondence has been preserved by the only child of Dugie and Dusty, Betty Lou Miller, who became a teacher—and a resourceful family historian.

Rocky did not think much of Sidney or Gladys or "Gran" (Nannie). Rocky was appalled at Gran's explosive fits of temper. "I shall remember to my dying day the first one I saw her pull." She felt that "there was some ugly blood" in Nannie's family and speculated on why Billy Johnson, whom she liked, married a bride who would cause domestic turmoil. Nannie and her family "always made such a sweet, goody, goody impression when in good humor, I suppose it was easy to fool a young boy in those days when there weren't many girls to choose from." Remembering the tragic death of her brother Cullen and the murder of Ed Sims in Snyder and the shootout in Sweetwater, Rocky was engulfed by dreadful recollections. "I some times think of the long ago as the most harrowing terrible dream imaginable; no wonder Grandad went crazy."[14]

Billy Johnson was not exactly crazy, but he sought medical and psychiatric help in San Antonio and Galveston, in addition to California. Finally Billy and Nannie moved back to Snyder. Nannie bought a comfortable house in Snyder and a shiny new car. While she pursued a pleasant lifestyle in Snyder, she sent her husband—who had accumulated the wealth that provided her house and auto—to be cared for by Trix. Of course, Billy probably found tranquility at the home of his favorite granddaughter. Wheelchair-bound by this time, Billy stayed outdoors on the porch or in the yard. Doctors ordered Billy not to smoke. But both Trix and her husband smoked, and Billy frequently sent his little grandson, Billy Bob McMullan, to smuggle cigarettes to him.[15]

Billy Johnson passed away at Trix's house on January 15, 1931. Just sixty-eight, it was felt within the family that Billy's health was broken and his life cut short by the youthful infidelities of Gladys and the humiliating tragedies of the feud. Funeral services were conducted the day after he died at the home of Trix and her family. As a teenaged cowboy, Billy Johnson had established his pioneer ranch more than a half a century earlier, and he was laid to rest in the Snyder Cemetery.[16]

Billy had written his will in 1920, naming his wife as executrix. The entire estate was designated as community property, and she did not probate the will until four years after his death. The value of their estate was estimated at $70,000, including a $15,000 residence in Altadena, California, and 215 shares of stock in the First National Bank of Snyder, valued at $5,000. The couple had divested themselves of all but two sections of the sprawling ranch that Billy had put together. At five dollars per acre, the 1,280 acres they retained were appraised at $6,400. Much of their property was sold to Sidney, who signed a note at six percent interest in 1925 for $65,000. It was due in 1935.[17]

Nannie remained in good health until early Saturday morning, December 17, 1938, when she died "after an illness of only a few hours." At seventy-four, Nannie was survived by two children, Sid and Gladys, as well as by seven grandchildren, four great-grandchildren, three sisters, and a brother. Sid had not yet paid off his $65,000 note, so in her will Nannie bequeathed Gladys $20,000 of this amount, to be paid within five years of her death. It is not believed that Sid ever paid Gladys.[18]

Sid owned twelve sections of the original Johnson ranch, including a house he built for $2,800 and the majestic home erected by his father. After Sid and his first wife, Ruth, divorced, he retained six sections, including the big house. On the first day of 1925 Sid married Clara Mae Beall, a schoolteacher from Ladonia in northeast Texas, and later in the year he bought twelve more sections of the Johnson ranch, thereby incurring the $65,000 debt.

Sid was a committed rancher who put the land to work in the best tradition of his father. Sid raised registered and commercial Herefords, which were shown at Fort Worth and at local stock shows.

Sid and Ruth Johnson built this ranch house for $2,800. In later years a wing was added to the rear, and the residence still is in use. Photo by the author.

He originated the Domino line of registered Herefords, and he was a member of the American Hereford Association and the Texas Hereford Association, as well as the Texas Southwestern Cattle Raisers Association. Clara showed sheep, which she had purchased with savings from her years as a teacher. Sid also raised cotton. During the Depression Sid and Clara had to sell all but twelve head of their cattle, both registered and commercial, but resolutely they rebuilt their herd.[19]

For all of his ability and accomplishments as a rancher, Sid remained a hard man to like. He drank heavily and had an explosive temper. He divorced his first wife, who had ridden horseback beside him while working their range, and who was the mother of his only child, Weldon. And he murdered his former brother-in-law with a shotgun on the Snyder square. On one drunken occasion in the big ranch house, Sid threw a china cabinet over the railing of the second-floor foyer onto the living area below. After another drinking bout he shot holes in the living room piano. Trix despised her uncle. "It has seemed for years, there was maddness [*sic*] smouldering between Sid and Trix," observed Rocky Higgins Johnson. "Those two have always wanted to kill each other . . . ." Sid seems to have inherited some of the "ugly blood" that Rocky felt ran in Nannie's family.[20]

Late in life Sid and Clara established a residence in San Antonio, while Clara's sister served as housekeeper of their big ranch home. On Thursday night, July 30, 1959, Sid—lubricated as usual with alcohol—was struck by a vehicle in San Antonio. He was rushed to a hospital, but died within a couple of hours.[21] Dead at sixty-nine, Sid was brought back to Snyder for services at the First Methodist Church and burial in the local cemetery. Sidney Johnson outlived Ed Sims by more than forty-two years.

The sister of Sid's widow somehow managed to attain title to the magnificent Johnson ranch home, along with six sections of land. Ownership of the historic house thus left the Johnson family, and today it stands empty, behind a locked gate.

Sid's son, Weldon, spent his life as a rancher. He married and had a son, Sidney Wallace Johnson. But like his father, Weldon was a heavy drinker. When he was seventy in 1984, his wife, Ida Sue Johnson, shot him in the head while he was in his pickup. She returned to their ranch house, called a granddaughter to tell her of the killing, then shot herself. The murder-suicide was yet another in the series of tragedies that plagued the Johnson family.[22]

The most painful tragedy suffered by Gladys Johnson Sims Hamer occurred during the last year of World War II. As the wife of a high profile lawman who had many enemies, Gladys was protective of her four children. They all grew up safely, and all four married and had children. Gladys was a devoted grandmother who extended her protectiveness to her grandchildren.

Grandson Billy Bob McMullan adored Gladys, calling her "gracious" and "a great lady." Billy Bob was well aware of the .44 automatic his grandmother carried in her purse. "We knew she'd use it on anyone who threatened us."[23]

When the United States entered World War II, Billy Bob was an underclassman at Snyder High School. Both Frank Hamer Jr. and Billy Hamer joined the U.S. Marines. Billy Bob wanted to enlist with Billy Hamer, but Trix McMullan—who had divorced Vern—informed her sixteen-year-old son that under no circumstances would she sign any permission papers for him to join the armed forces. So Billy Bob played football for the Snyder Tigers and graduated from Snyder High School in 1944, then joined the Army Air Corps. By that time Frank Hamer Jr. was a Marine pilot, while Billy Hamer was in combat in the Pacific.[24]

Billy Hamer was part of the Marine invasion force that assaulted Iwo Jima in February 1945. They met ferocious resistance, and Billy Hamer became one of nearly 6,000 Marines slain on the strategic island. Another 17,000 Americans were wounded, while nearly all of the 22,000 Japanese defenders died. The Hamers did not receive word of Billy's death from the War Department until May.[25] Frank and Gladys were staggered by the loss of their youngest son, but they both were from tough frontier stock, and with somber resolve they carried on, like so many other wartime parents.

Billy Hamer, youngest son of Frank and
Gladys, in his Marine khakis on a visit home
during World War II. Billy was killed at Iwo
Jima in 1945. Courtesy Beverly Sims.

It was sadly ironic that three decades earlier Gladys and Sid had shot Ed Sims, depriving Laura Belle Sims of a son. Now Gladys suffered the same tragic loss, although she had the consolation that Billy Hamer had died a hero's death in defense of his country.

After Frank Hamer died in 1955, Gladys continued to live in their house on Riverside Drive in Austin. She slept with her .44 automatic under her pillow, and kept it with her wherever she went. One night she was reading in a chair in her living room when a man peered in her window. Gladys immediately picked up her .44 and triggered a shot through the window, sending the Peeping Tom fleeing into the darkness.[26]

Gladys suffered another terrible loss in 1966 when her oldest daughter died in a fire at her ranch house. Fifty-seven-year-old Helen Trix Sims—she had taken her maiden name back after divorcing Vern McMullan—was alone when her home was demolished on the night of April 12. It was speculated that the fire may have started because Trix was smoking in bed. Trix was buried in her yard, a short distance from the front porch of her ruined house.[27]

Now seventy-five, Gladys did not make the trip from Austin. Two of her four children were gone, along with her husband and all three of her brothers and, of course, her parents. Although Frank Jr. lived nearby, Beverly usually lived outside of Texas, and the last decade of Gladys's life must have been lonely. Gladys died in 1976 at eighty-five. All of her family, including grandchildren and great-grandchildren, gathered to see her laid to rest beside her beloved Frank in Austin Memorial Park.

Her grandson, Billy Bob McMullan, stayed in Snyder and exhibited the best qualities of his pioneer ancestors. Discharged from the Army Air Corps in 1947, he used the GI Bill to attend Texas Tech, graduating four years later with a degree in animal husbandry. He taught agriculture for thirty-five years, all but one at Snyder High School. For decades he daily exerted a positive influence on the adolescent students of his home town. Billy Bob married and had four

Billy Bob McMullan standing before the ruins of the house where he was raised. His parents' bedroom is behind him, the living room and fireplace are beyond, and to the right is the front porch. The house was destroyed by fire in 1966, killing his mother, Trix Sims.

Trix Sims was buried near her house; her shrouded marker is in the foreground. The gravestone marks the burial site of Trix's daughter, Ann Brunson, who died of cancer at sixty-three in 1993. Photo by the author.

daughters, and he remains an active member of the Methodist Church his Johnson great-grandparents founded.

Raised on a ranch, Billy Bob ranched on the side throughout his teaching career. He inherited the half-section where his boyhood home stood, and he bought one section of McMullan land. The half-section that Trix was given by her grandparents, and that Billy Bob works to this day, is the only parcel of the forty-seven contiguous sections amassed by Billy Johnson that remains in the possession of a Johnson descendant. Now in his eighties, Billy Bob McMullan drives from Snyder to his ranching operation almost every day, checking his cattle and land and fencing. He is fit and energetic, amiable and even-tempered. A lifelong rancher, he is devoted to the heritage of the once-great spread to which he alone is a working heir. The blood of the Johnsons and the Sims runs in his veins, and Billy Bob McMullan is a credit to both families.[28]

Billy Bob's contemporary and distant cousin, Ed Sims, now in his eighties, likewise became an exemplary citizen and an active rancher. Futhermore, Ed was a noted Professional Rodeo Cowboys Association rodeo champion and a master spur maker who found an unexpected measure of distinction. Ed's father, U. B. "Kelly" Sims, was the fourth child and second son of Dave and Laura Belle. Like his father, Kelly was born in a covered wagon during the family move to West Texas in 1888.

In 1915 Kelly married Lora Nance, called "Sweet," of Justiceburg, fifteen miles southeast of Post and about ten miles west of the Sims ranch. Kelly inherited and purchased twelve sections, and his ranching activities always included roundups at the old home ranch and drives to the railroad stock pens at Justiceburg.

Kelly and Sweet had a daughter, Lucille, and, on the first day of 1924, a son who was the namesake of Kelly's lamented older brother, Ed Kelly Sims. Ed Kelly grew up on a pony with a rope in his hand. He helped with the Sims home ranch roundups and rode horseback to rural schools. Then the family built a house in Post, for $3,300, and Sweet spent school weeks in town while Lucille and Ed Kelly went to

Young cowboy Ed Sims with his mother, Sweet. The Sims family built a town house in Post so that Ed and his sister, Lucille, could attend school in Post, while returning to the family ranch on weekends, holidays and summers. Courtesy Ed Sims.

the big school in the south part of Post. On weekends and during the summers the family was together on their ranch west of Justiceburg.

An expert roper, Ed Kelly began entering area rodeo competitions as a youngster. Soon he joined the professional circuit. During his career he won more than eighty events, earning a gold PRCA card. Ed Kelly began making his own spurs, exhibiting an artistic flair for design. Other rodeo men noticed and wanted similar spurs for themselves. Deciding to invest in his cowboy craft, Ed ordered one hundred pairs from a foundry.

"I'll never sell these!" he told his wife Anne, who had grown up in Post across the street from Ed, and who developed a schoolgirl crush on the handsome young cowboy.

But Ed and Anne sold thirty-eight pairs of spurs at the first rodeo after the spurs were delivered. Soon they decided to make a serious commitment to spur-making. Ed sold his cattle herd to raise $175,000 for machinery. A factory was established in Uvalde, where they already owned property. They sold $19,000 worth of spurs during the first year of operations, $43,000 worth during the second year, and $70,000 worth the third year.

There were ten employees at the factory and seventeen salesmen, who had little trouble selling Ed's eye-catching designs. Ed fashioned spurs for Gene Autry, Reba McEntire, Nick Nolte, Charlie Daniels, James Drury, Ethan Wayne, and many other actors, singers, and other Western celebrities. Of course, the entire rodeo world wanted Ed's spurs, and sales eventually reached one million dollars annually. But Ed's spurs were so popular that foreign companies with cheap labor would copy new designs within weeks. Steel bills and taxes mounted, and in time Ed and Anne decided to close their business. But by then 40,000 pairs of uniquely impressive Ed Sims spurs were in circulation.[29]

Ed and Anne moved back to Post. Anne has a real estate agency, and every day Ed drives to work at their ranch north of town. Ed and Anne proudly maintain documents and artifacts and stories about their family history. Likeable and friendly, Ed in earlier years found

Namesake of an ill-fated uncle, and a cowboy since boyhood, Ed Sims carried the ranching traditions of his family to new dimensions. Courtesy Ed and Anne Sims.

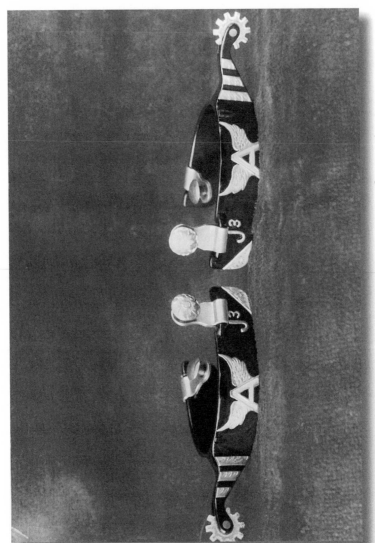

Ed Sims crafted this set of spurs for Gene Autry, featuring Autry's famous Flying A. Courtesy Ed Sims.

Nick Nolte, while starring as a contemporary
Texas Ranger in the 1987 motion picture,
Extreme Prejudice, received a personalized set
of spurs from Ed Sims. Courtesy Ed Sims.

fellow rancher Weldon Johnson congenial. Ed Sims and the son of Sidney Johnson developed an unlikely friendship, symbolic in small measure to the reconciliation of the Capulets and Montagues.

The Johnson and Sims ranch houses still stand on their original sites, although both historic homes have fallen out of family ownership. Billy Johnson's old First National Bank building also still stands, overlooking the street where Ed Sims was shot by Gladys and Sid. The law office of Cullen Higgins was upstairs, and his last home continues to be part of a Snyder neighborhood.

Beverly Sims Benson, daughter of Gladys and Ed, is approaching her centennial birthday—bright and charming and devoid of bitterness about the blood feud that embroiled both sides of her family. Beverly's nephew, Billy Bob McMullan, still ranches a parcel of the original Johnson spread, while the namesake of Ed Sims also remains an active rancher. Neither man maintains a shred of the hard feelings that once wracked their families. Indeed, throughout their long lives both men have brought credit to their families.

Although there are tangible remains of the Johnson-Sims families, and although direct descendants still live and ranch in the old regions, the murderous spirit of the last blood feud in Texas has long vanished.

Rest in Peace

1915   Lee Rasberry, shot by Joshua Bostick in Rotan

1916   Joshua Bostick, shot by Will Luman in countryside
Ed Sims, 32, shot by ex-wife and Sid Johnson in Snyder

1917   Gee McMeans, shot by Frank Hamer in Sweetwater

1918   Cullen Higgins, 42, assassinated in Claremont
Si Bostick, "suicide" in Sweetwater jail

1919   Dave Sims, 61, died of cancer at ranch house

1927   Emmett Johnson, 41, accidentally shot near Wichita Falls

1931   W. A. "Billy" Johnson, 68, died at daughter's ranch

1938   Nannie Johnson, 74, died in Snyder

1955   Frank Hamer, 71, died in Austin

1956   Laura Belle Sims, 91, died in Post

1959   Sid Johnson, 68, killed by automobile in San Antonio

1966   Trix Sims, 57, killed in fire at her ranch house

1976   Gladys Johnson Sims Hamer, 85, died in Austin

Endnotes

Notes to Chapter 1

1. The shooting of Ed Sims is described in the *Snyder Signal,* December 22, 1916, and testimony of the subsequent examining trial is printed verbatim in this same issue.
2. The only book-length treatment of the Regulator-Moderator War was published by the East Texas Historical Association in 2006: O'Neal, *War in East Texas, Regulators vs. Moderators.*
3. These feuds were explored by C. L Sonnichsen in *I'll Die Before I'll Run* and *Ten Texas Feuds.*
4. Two recent investigations of the Sutton-Taylor feud are Parsons, *The Sutton-Taylor Feud,* and Smallwood, *The Feud That Wasn't.*
5. For the Horrell-Higgins Feud, see Nolan, *Bad Blood,* and O'Neal, *Pink Higgins.* For the Mason County War, see Johnson, *The Mason County "Hoo Doo" War.*
6. Sonnichsen, *I'll Die Before I'll Run* and *Ten Texas Feuds.*
7. Sonnichsen, *I'll Die Before I'll Run,* explores both the Jaybird-Woodpecker War and the Wall-Border-Broocks Feud. For the latter feud, also see Combs, *Gunsmoke in the Redlands.* Useful for the Jaybird-Woodpecker War is Yelderman's *The Jay Bird Democratic Association of Fort Bend County.*
8. The quotes in this and the following two paragraphs are taken from essays Doc Sonnichsen wrote about feuding in *I'll Die Before I Run,* 3–11 and 316–324, and in *Ten Texas Feuds,* 3–8. During the late 1980s I was privileged to associate with Doc, who discussed with me feuding in general and the Horrell-Higgins conflict in particular.
9. O'Neal, *Fighting Men of the Indian Wars,* 4–6, 20–35.
10. O'Neal, *Encyclopedia of Western Gunfighters.*
11. Shakespeare, *Romeo and Juliet,* prologue and act 3, scene 1.
12. Shakespeare, *Romeo and Juliet,* act 3, scene 1

Notes to Chapter 2

1. Fehrenbach, *Lone Star,* 554; Frantz, *Texas,* 127.
2. Fehrenbach, *Lone Star,* 560, 561.

3. Hunter, ed., *Trail Drivers of Texas*, 597.
4. Census of 1860 and 1880, Gonzales County, Texas; *Gonzales County Brand and Mark Book; Gonzales Inquirer,* June 2, 1882.
5. For general information on Gonzales County, see *History of Gonzales County*.
6. Hunter, ed., *Trail Drivers of Texas*, 597–601; Mellard, *Dream of a Youthful Cowboy*, 2–6.
7. Lois Lucie Curnutte, whose father was a bank employee and "close friend" of Billy Johnson, wrote one of the most useful articles on Johnson: "W. A. Johnson–A Man for His Time," *First Cattlemen On the Lower Plains of Texas*, 13–16. Also see Chamblin, ed., *Historical Encyclopedia of Texas*, "Sidney Johnson," 1061.
8. Shelton, comp., *From Buffalo to Oil*, 11–15.
9. Nunn quote in ibid., 23.
10. "Weldon and Ida Sue Johnson," *Footprints Across Scurry County*, 305.
11. *Footprints Across Scurry County*, 28.
12. Hunter, ed., *Trail Drivers of Texas,* 600–601.
13. Curnutte, "W. A. Johnson," *First Cattlemen*, 13.
14. Ibid.
15. *Footprints Across Scurry County*, 32–33.
16. "Scurry County," *First Annual Report of the Agricultural Bureau,* 200–201.
17. Curnutte, "W. A. Johnson," *First Cattlemen*, 15.
18. Ibid. Sidney Johnson recalled going to grade school at the Ennis Creek School. "Sidney Johnson," *Historical Encyclopedia of Texas*, 1061.
19. Curnutte, "W. A. Johnson," *First Cattlemen,* 15.
20. "Sidney Johnson," *Historical Encyclopedia of Texas*, 1061.
21. Curnutte, "W. A. Johnson," *First Cattlemen*, 14.
22. *The Coming West,* October 18, 1900.
23. *Footprints Across Scurry County*, 30, 34.
24. Ibid., 269–282.

Notes to Chapter 3

1. A great deal of information about the family of Dave Sims was compiled onto a concentrated genealogy sheet by Lucille Sims Richards of Post.
2. Census of 1860, Lampasas County.
3. Lampasas History Book Committee, *Lampasas County*, 346.
4. Ibid., 346, 417–418, 420–421.
5. Ibid., 158.
6. John Nichols, interview by J. Evetts Haley, 7–8.

7. The only book-length biography of Higgins is O'Neal, *Pink Higgins*.
8. Information about Dandy Jim and Sarah James Smith was compiled by Emma Smith in "James Gibson Smith," *Burnet County History*, ed. Darrell Debo, vol. 1, 282–284. Also see Census of 1870 and 1880, Burnet County.
9. Sparks, "A Winner of the West," *Frontier Times*, vol. 16, no. 7 (April 1939); Stokes, *Paisano*.
10. *Lampasas County, Texas*, 346.
11. Sims genealogy by Lucille Sims Terry.
12. "Mills County," *First Annual Report of the Agricultural Bureau*, 160–161.
13. Ibid.
14. The family stories about Laura Belle Sims buying Kent County land through a lawyer from Austin and about the OXO herd being turned back at the New Mexico line were told to me on several occasions by Ed Sims of Post.
15. The size of the Sims ranch and the rule of thumb regarding cattle per section were related to me by Ed Sims of Post.
16. Ed Sims described the buildings of the home ranch, and on May 20, 2008, I was conducted on a tour of these structures by Larry Rapier, the current ranch foreman.
17. Ed and Anna Sims of Post showed me the fiddle and its case, and told me the story of Dave Sims and the starving family.
18. Clairemont is described in *The New Texas Handbook*, vol. 2, 127–128. Also see Geeslin, *Kent County, 1892–1992*.
19. Sims genealogy by Lucille Sims Terry.
20. Fehrenbach, *Lone Star*, 301–302.

Notes to Chapter 4

1. Curnutte, "W. A. Johnson," *First Cattlemen*, 14–15.
2. Beverly Sims Benson, interview.
3. Information about Emmett and Sid at New Mexico Military Institute provided to the author by NMMI Registrar Ed Preble and Alumni Director Renee James-Bressen. Roll books, 1905–1906, and Yearbook, 1905–1906.
4. Kidd-Key College Records and Yearbook, 1904–1905. Southern Methodist University Archives, Dallas. W. A. Johnson was charged not quite $400 for his daughter's year at college.
5. Mellard, *Dream of a Youthful Cowboy*, 22–23.
6. Case No. 76, District Court of Garza County. *E. C. Sims vs. Gladys Sims*, July 25, 1916.

7. Sims genealogy by Lucille Sims Terry; Census of 1910, El Paso County; handwritten list of early Ector County law officers in local history section, Odessa Public Library.

8. Shakespeare, *Romeo and Juliet*, act 1, scene 2.

9. Wedding certificate, September 7, 1905, Scurry County.

10. Case No. 76, District Court of Garza County. *E. C. Sims vs. Gladys Sims*, July 25, 1916.

11. *Ibid.*

12. The story of C. W. Post and the founding of Post City are detailed in Eaves and Hutchison, *Post City, Texas.*

13. Rocky Higgins and Emmett Johnson, wedding invitation, author's collection.

14. For this period of Pink's life, see O'Neal, *Pink Higgins*, 60–75.

15. J. P. Higgins, Certificate of Prison Conduct, December 3, 1893; interview with Jeff Jackson, Lampasas historian, September 29, 1998.

16. Dr. John Higgins of Lampasas told the author about the sojourn in East Texas during which Cullen and Tom Higgins attended business colleges. Tom's obituary lists his matriculation at Tyler Commercial College and at "summer normals" for teachers.

17. O'Neal, *Pink Higgins*, 72–79.

18. Dr. John Higgins of Lampasas offered the author these conclusions about Cullen's preparation for the bar and early career.

19. Holt, *The District Courts of Scurry County and Their Presiding Judges*, "Judge Cullen Higgins."

20. Pritchett and Black, *Kent County and Its People*, 204.

21. *Snyder Signal,* March 22, 1918.

22. Correspondence between Rocky and Emmett was loaned to the author by their granddaughter, Betty Miller Giddens. The sweethearts wrote frequently in 1905, 1906, and 1907.

23. Wedding invitation for Rocky and Emmett loaned to the author by Betty Miller Giddens. Also see *Snyder Signal,* May 19, 1927.

24. "Sidney Johnson," *Historical Encyclopedia of Texas,* 1061.

25. For a description of the Johnson ranch house and its construction, see "'Elegant' Johnson home built on August, 1910," *Snyder Daily News,* February 12, 1995.

26. Beverly Sims Benson, interview.

Notes to Chapter 5

1. Case No. 76, District Court of Garza County. *E. C. Sims vs. Gladys Sims*, July 25, 1916.

2. Ibid.

3.   Ibid.

4.   Ibid.

5.   Beverly Sims Benson, interview.

6.   Case No. 76, District Court of Garza County. *E. C. Sims vs. Gladys Sims*, July 25, 1916. The visit to Presidio County is recounted primarily in the "Interrogatories" and "Cross-interrogatories" submitted to Garland Mellard by the opposing attorneys. Mellard answered the questions in Marfa on June 9, 1916, before K. C. Miller, Notary Public. The trip to Marfa also is discussed by Ed on pages 15 and 27–28 of the divorce testimony.

7.   Case No. 76, District Court of Garza County. *E. C. Sims vs. Gladys Sims*, July 25, 1916.

8.   Ibid.

9.   Ibid.

10. Ibid.

11. Ibid.

12. Mrs. Dorsey's journey to and from West Texas is detailed in the Interrogatories and Cross-interrogatories of Mrs. Drusilla Dorsey for Case No. 76. Mrs. Dorsey responded to the questions from the lawyers of Ed and Gladys in Dallas on June 24, 1916, before Paul J. Robertson, Notary Public.

13. Ibid.

14. Case No. 76, District Court of Garza County, *E. C. Sims vs. Gladys Sims*, July 25, 1916.

15. Estate of E. C. Sims Deceased, *Garza County Probate Minutes*, February 14, 1917.

16. Case No. 76, District Court of Garza County, *E. C. Sims vs. Gladys Sims*, July 25, 1916.

17. Ibid.; Beverly Sims Benson, interview; Case No. 1825, District Court of Scurry County, *Gladys (Johnson) Sims vs. Ed Sims*, May 6, 1916.

18. Case No. 76, District Court of Garza County, *E. C. Sims vs. Gladys Sims*, July 25, 1916.

19. E. C. Sims, Last Will and Testament, Filed in Garza County Probate Court on February 14, 1917.

20. *Sweetwater Daily Reporter*, July 31, 1916; Case No. 1825, District Court of Scurry County, *Gladys (Johnson) Sims vs. Ed Sims*, order of Judge John B. Thomas, June 27, 1916.

21. The armed confrontation in Post City is described in a *Post City Post* article reprinted in the *Sweetwater Daily Reporter*, July 31, 1916.

22. Case No. 1825, District Court of Scurry County, *Gladys (Johnson) Sims vs. Ed Sims*, September term, 1916.

Notes to Chapter 6

1. In 1964, nine years after Frank Hamer's death, biographical research was begun by H. Gordon Frost and John H. Jenkins, with the full cooperation of Gladys Hamer and other family members. *"I'm Frank Hamer"* was published in 1968.
2. Frost and Jenkins, *"I'm Frank Hamer,"* 268.
3. Frank Hamer, Enlistment Papers, Texas Ranger Hall of Fame Library.
4. Harrison F. Hamer, interview; and Harrison F. Hamer, *Hamer Brothers: Texas Rangers*, DVD.
5. Webb, *Texas Rangers*, 530, 546.
6. Beverly Sims Benson, interview.
7. A two-part autobiographical article about Luman—"Trailing Up Cow Thieves," by Bill (Dutch) Luman, as told to Jane Pattie—appeared in *The Cattleman* in 1878. In addition to this useful source, there is a file on Luman in the library of the Southwestern Cattle Raisers Association in Fort Worth. The author also enjoyed two informative interviews with Gene and Wyvonne Kennedy of Post; Gene is the nephew of Will Luman, while Wyvonne is an extremely well informed family historian.
8. Luman and Pattie, "Trailing Up Cow Thieves," part 1, *The Catttleman*, 86, and part 2, 70.
9. Case No. 166, District Court of Kent County. *State of Texas vs. Lee Rasberry* for cattle theft. There are 130 pages of testimony, which provide most of the details used by the author in describing this incident.
10. Case No. 820, District Court of Fisher County. *State of Texas vs. Will Luman* for murder, 113 and 121.
11. Case No. 3291, Texas State Court of Appeals. Appeal from Jones County, Lee Rasberry, Appellant. *Abilene Reporter*, March 6, 1916.
12. The long-told story about Rasberry writing Joshua Bostick and Sidney Johnson was related to me by Kinnith Hardin of Rotan and Bob Terry of Roby, who also both described to me the subsequent shooting in Rotan.
13. Case No. 820, 113.
14. Case No. 820, 123.
15. *Abilene Reporter*, March 6, 1916; *Snyder Signal*, March 10, 1916. These two newspapers offered accounts of the shooting and aftermath, in addition to the accounts in the lengthy trial testimony in Case No. 820.
16. The two-year history of the case against Rasberry and Luman may be traced through the numerous documents in the file of Case No. 820. Luman's arrest is described in the *Snyder Signal* of May 18, 1917,

and in his testimony in Case No. 820. I couldn't erase one of the hard
returns in this note without doing strange things to the note number

Notes to Chapter 7

1. Case No. 644, District Court of Scurry County. *State of Texas vs. Sidney Johnson* for murder.
2. Beverly Sims Benson, interview.
3. The events of Friday night and Saturday, December 15 and 16, 1916, are described in the *Snyder Signal*, December 22, 1916. Many details are provided in the testimony of the hearing of Monday, December 18. The hearing documents disappeared from the courthouse, but the testimony was reprinted verbatim in the *Snyder Signal*, December 22, 1916.
4. *Snyder Signal*, December 22, 1916.
5. *Snyder Signal*, December 22, 1916.
6. *Snyder Signal*, December 22, 1916.
7. Beverly Sims Benson, interview.
8. *Snyder Signal*, December 22, 1916.
9. *Snyder Signal*, December 22, 1916.
10. Case No. 644, District Court of Scurry County. *State of Texas vs. Sidney Johnson* for murder.
11. Frost and Jenkins, "*I'm Frank Hamer,*" 67; Beverly Sims Benson, interview.

Notes to Chapter 8

1. *Snyder Signal*, December 22, 1916.
2. The telegram is quoted in the *Snyder Signal*, December 22, 1916.
3. Frost and Jenkins, "*I'm Frank Hamer,*" 67–68.
4. Frank Hamer quoted in Frost and Jenkins, "*I'm Frank Hamer,*" 68–69.
5. Frank and Harrison Hamer related this incident as recounted in Frost and Jenkins, "*I'm Frank Hamer,*" 68–70.
6. Case No. 645, District Court of Scurry County. *State of Texas vs. Sidney Johnson* for murder. Case No. 140, District Court of Dawson County. *State of Texas vs. Gladys Sims* for assault with intent. Criminal Minutes, District Court, vol. 1.
7. Case No. 1794, District Court of Callahan County. *State of Texas vs. Sidney Johnson* for murder.
8. Frank Hamer Jr. assured the author that the street fight in Sweetwater occurred exactly as described in "*I'm Frank Hamer,*" 70–73. Also see the account in the *Dallas Morning News*, September 18, 1917.
9. Frost and Jenkins, "*I'm Frank Hamer,*" 71–72.

10. Frost and Jenkins, *"I'm Frank Hamer,"* 72.
11. Frank Hamer Jr. related to the author family stories of the 1917–1918 sojourn in California. Also see Frost and Jenkins, *"I'm Frank Hamer,"* 74–80.

Notes to Chapter 9

1. Case No 246, District Court of Kent County. S*tate of Texas vs. R. N. Higdon* for murder. S. D. Sims and J. A. Durham were the two sureties for "the penal sum of $10,000" for Higdon, permitting his release from custody pending his appearance two months later in court.
2. The *Snyder Signal*, March 22, 1918, reported a detailed account of the death and burial of Cullen Higgins. Later editions described the arrests of Si Bostick, Bob Higdon, and Will Luman.
3. *Snyder Signal*, March 22, 1918.
4. *Sweetwater Daily Republic*, March 23, 1918.
5. Pink Terry related to his son, Bob Terry, and to the author, among others, the discovery of the shotgun.
6. District Court Records of Kent County: Indictments of R. N. Higdon and Will Luman, Grand Jury, Special Term, March 1918.
7. District Court Records of Kent County: R. N. Higdon, Habeas Corpus application, May 3, 1918; Cause No. 246, *State of Texas vs. R. N. Higdon*, September 23, 1918; Cause No. 247, *State of Texas vs. Will Luman*, September 23, 1918.
8. District Court Records of Haskell County: Case No. 1157, *State of Texas vs. Will Luman*, November 12, 1917– May 22, 1919; Case No. 1233, *State of Texas vs. Will Luman*, May 5, 1919–December 10, 1919; *State of Texas vs. R. N. Higdon*, May 5, 1919–December 10, 1919.
9. Interview with Gene and Wyvonne Kennedy in Post, May 20, 2008. Gene is Will Luman's nephew.
10. The archives of the Southwestern Cattle Raisers Association have an employee file on Will Luman. Also see Luman, "Trailing Up Cattle Thieves," *The Cattleman*, April and May, 1978.
11. Case No. 1794, District Court of Callahan County: *State of Texas vs. Sidney Johnson* for murder.
12. *Snyder Signal*, May 31 and June 8, 1918. The suit was "Continued by agreement" and settled out of court. But this legal annoyance in Snyder was one additional public embarrassment for Billy Johnson.
13. Curnutte, "W. A. Johnson," *First Cattlemen*.
14. Terri Laurence, deputy clerk of Garza County, located a handwritten death record for Dave Sims in a "death book."

Notes to Chapter 10

1. Ed Sims, interview; Billy Bob McMullan, interview.
2. Frank Hamer, Inactive Personnel Record, Texas Ranger Hall of Fame Library, Waco; Webb, *Texas Rangers*, 519, 529–533.
3. Beverly Sims Benson, interview.
4. Beverly Sims Benson, interview.
5. Frank Hamer Jr., interview.
6. Beverly Sims Benson, interview.
7. Beverly Sims Benson, interview.
8. Billy Bob McMullan, interview.
9. Billy Bob McMullan, interview.
10. Ed Sims, interview.
11. Frost and Jenkins, *"I'm Frank Hamer,"* 249–255.
12. Obituary, *Snyder Signal*, May 19, 1927; Rocky Higgins to Nannie Johnson, May 14, 1927; Betty Miller Giddens, interview.
13. Obituary, *Snyder Signal,* May 19, 1927.
14. Rocky Higgins to Dugie Miller, September 1, 1935.
15. Billy Bob McMullan, interview; Beverly Sims Benson, interview.
16. Obituary, *Scurry County Times*, January 22, 1931.
17. Last Will and Testament of W. A. Johnson, November 27, 1920; Appraisal and Probate documents, No. 669, February 13 and March 30, 1931.
18. Obituary, *Scurry County Times*, December 22, 1938; Last Will and Testament of Nannie May Johnson, July 18, 1933; Codicil, July 26, 1937; Probate documents, No. 938, September 11, 1938; Beverly Sims Benson, interview.
19. Chamblin, ed., *Historical Encyclopedia of Texas*, "Sidney Johnson," 1061.
20. Sidney's drunken behavior was known by the family and many others. The two incidents in the ranch house were related to me by family members Betty Miller Giddens, who has kept the only two unbroken pieces of china as heirlooms, and Billy Bob McMullan, who regarded Sid as "self-centered" and "bad-tempered." Rocky Higgins to Dugie Miller, September 1, 1935.
21. Obituaries, *Snyder Daily News*, July 31 and August 2, 1959.
22. *Snyder Daily News*, September 24, 1984.
23. Billy Bob McMullan, interview.
24. Billy Bob McMullan, interview.
25. Frost and Jenkins, *"I'm Frank Hamer,"* 270.
26. Billy Bob McMullan, interview.

27. *Abilene Reporter-News*, April 13, 1966, and *San Angelo Standard Times*, April 12, 1966.
28. Billy Bob McMullan, interview.
29. The account of Ed Kelly Sims is based on multiple interviews with Ed and Anne Sims at their home in Post.

Bibliography

Documents and Legal Records

Callahan County District Court Records. Baird, Texas.
Dawson County District Court Records. Lamesa, Texas.
Fisher County District Court Records. Roby, Texas.
Garza County Probate Minutes, 1917, E. C. Sims estate. Post, Texas.
Haskell County District Court Records. Haskell, Texas.
Jones County District Court Records. Anson, Texas.
Kent County District Court Records. Jayton, Texas.
Lampasas County District Court Records. Lampasas, Texas.
Scurry County District Court Records. Snyder, Texas.
Scurry County Marriage Record Book I, 23 August 1884 to 19 April 1907. Snyder,
    Texas.
Scurry County Probate Court, 1931, W. A. Johnson estate, and 1939, Nannie May
    Johnson estate. Snyder, Texas.

Federal Census Records

Burnet County: 1870, 1880
El Paso County: 1910
Gonzales County: 1860, 1880
Kent County: 1890, 1900
Lampasas County: 1860, 1870, 1880
Presidio County: 1910
Scurry County: 1890, 1900, 1910, 1920
Travis County: 1930

Published Primary Sources

Foster, L. L. Commissioner. *Forgotten Texas Census: First Annual Report of the
    Agricultural Bureau of the Department or Agriculture, Insurance, Statistics, and
    History. 1887–88.* Austin: State Printing Office, 1889. Reprint by Texas State
    Historical Association, Austin, 2001.
Frost, H. Gordon, and John H. Jenkins. *"I'm Frank Hamer": The Life of Texas Peace
    Officer.* Austin: Pemberton Press, 1968.
Hunter, J. Marvin, ed. *The Trail Drivers of Texas.* Austin: University of Texas Press,
    1992.

Jones, Charles Adam. "Pink Higgins, The Good Bad Man." *Atlantic Monthly* (July 1934): 79–89.

Luman, Bill (Dutch), as told to Jane Pattie. "Trailing Up Cow Thieves," parts 1 and 2. *The Cattleman* (April 1978): 40ff. and (May 1978): 56ff.

Mellard, Frank Courtney. *The Dream of a Youthful Cowboy.* [Marfa, Texas]: Big Bend Sentinel, 1957.

Parks, Aline, and Dudley Cramer, eds. *First Cattlemen On The Lower Plains of West Texas.* Snyder, Texas: Ranch Headquarters Association, 1971.

Newspapers

Abilene Reporter
Austin Daily Journal
Dallas Morning News
Gonzales Inquirer
San Angelo Standard Times
Scurry County Times
Snyder Daily News
Snyder Signal
Sweetwater Daily Reporter
Texas Spur

Unpublished Materials

Correspondence between Rocky Higgins and Emmett Johnson, 1905–1907. Betty L. Giddens, Clyde, Texas.

Correspondence between Rocky Higgins Johnson and her children, 1932–1954. Betty L. Giddens, Clyde, Texas.

Gonzales County Brand and Mark Book. Gonzales, Texas.

Hamer, Frank, Enlistment Papers and Inactive Personnel Record. Texas Ranger Hall of Fame Library, Waco.

Higgins, J. P., Certificate of Prison Conduct, December 3, 1893. Texas State Archives, Austin.

Jones, Clifford B. "Notes on the Life of 'Pink' Higgins." Unpublished typescript.

List of early Ector County law officers, Odessa Public Library.

Luman, Will. Personnel File, Southwestern Cattle Raisers Association archives, Fort Worth.

Price, Margaret Ann. "From Rails to Rigs: The Early History of Ector County, Texas, 1881–1927." Master's Thesis, University of Texas Permian, 1977.

Records and yearbook, 1904–1905, Kidd-Key College. Southern Methodist University Archives, Dallas.

Richards, Lucille Sims. Samuel David Sims genealogy sheet.

Roll book and yearbook, 1905–1906. New Mexico Military Institute archives, Roswell, New Mexico.

Spur Ranch Records, vol. 10, Correspondence, 1899–1903. Southwest Collection, Texas Tech University, Lubbock, Texas.

Wedding certificate, Samuel David Sims and Laura Belle Smith, January 7, 1882, Burnet County, Texas.

Wedding invitation, Rocky Higgins and Emmett Johnson. Copy in owner's collection.

Interviews

Benson, Beverly Sims, interviewed by author, San Marcos, Texas, March 2008.

Giddens, Betty Miller, numerous interviews by author, Clyde and Fort Worth, Texas, 1997–2009.

Hamer, Frank, Jr., telephone interviews by author, San Marcos, Texas, March 1997.

Hamer, Harrison F., interviewed by author, San Marcos, Texas, March 2008.

Hardin, Kinnith, interviewed by author, Rotan, Texas, June 1997.

Higgins, Dr. John, interviewed by author, Lampasas, Texas, March 1997.

Jackson, Jeff, interviewed by author, Lampasas, Texas, June 1997.

Kennedy, Gene, and Wyvonne Kennedy, interviewed by author, Post, Texas, April 2008.

McMullan, Billy Bob, interviewed by author, Snyder, Texas, November 2008.

Nichols, John, interviewed by J. Evetts Haley, May 15, 1927. Haley Library and History Center, Midland, Texas.

Sims, Ed, and Anne Sims, multiple interviews by author, 2008.

Terry, Bob, numerous interviews by author, Roby, Texas, 1997–2009.

Secondary Sources

Anderson, Charles G. *Reflections, An Album of West Texas History, 1840–1990*. Snyder, Texas: Scurry County Historical Commission, 1990.

Chamblin, Thomas S., ed. *The Historical Encyclopedia of Texas*. 2 vols. Austin: Historical Institute, 1982.

Combs, Joseph F. *Gunsmoke in the Redlands*. San Antonio: Naylor Company, 1968.

Debo, Darrell, ed. *Burnet County History*, 2 vols. Burnet, Texas: Eakin Press, 1979.

Garza County Historical Association. *Wagon Wheels: A History of Garza County*. Edited by Charles Didway. Burnet, Texas: Eakin Publications, 1980.

Douglas, C. L. *Famous Texas Feuds*. Dallas: Turner Company, 1936.

Eaves, Charles Dudley, and C. A. Hutchinson. *Post City, Texas: C. W. Post's Colonizing Activities in West Texas*. 1952 edition reprinted by Maxine Durrett Earl Charitable Foundation, 1998.

Elliott, W. J. *The Spurs*. [Spur, Texas]: Texas Spur, 1939.

Fehrenbach. T. R. *Lone Star, A History of Texas and the Texans*. New York: Macmillan, 1968.

Frantz, Joe B. *Texas, A Bicentennial History*. New York: W. W. Norton, 1976.

Galusha, Bill. *C. W. Post, The Man—The Legend*. Slaton, Texas: Brazos Offset Printers, n.d.

Gard, Wayne. *Frontier Justice*. Norman: University of Oklahoma Press, 1949.

Geeslin, Mark A. *Kent County, 1892–1992*. N.p., 1992.

Gonzales County Historical Commission. *History of Gonzales County*. Dallas: Curtis Publishing Company, 1986.

Holden, William Curry. *The Espuela Land and Cattle Company*. Austin: Texas State Historical Association, 1970.

Holt, Wayland G. *The District Courts of Scurry County and Their Presiding Judges: The First One Hundred Years*. Snyder, Texas: Scurry County Historical Commission, 1985.

Johnson, David. *The Mason County "Hoo Doo" War, 1874–1902*. Denton: University of North Texas Press, 2006.

Lampasas History Book Committee, comps. *Lampasas County, Texas: Its History and Its People*. Marceline, Missouri: Walsworth Publishing Company, 1991.

Kinney, Harrison. "Frank Hamer, Texas Ranger." *American Gun* (February 1961): 82–89.

Mellard, Evelyn. *Spur Ranch–and Other Circles of Time*. Salado, Texas: Anson Jones Press, 1977.

Nolan, Frederick. *Bad Blood: The Life and Times of the Horrell Brothers*. Stillwater, Oklahoma: Barbed Wire Press, 1994.

O'Neal, Bill. *The Bloody Legacy of Pink Higgins: A Half Century of Violence in Texas*. Austin: Eakin Press, 1999.

———*Encyclopedia of Western Gunfighters*. Norman: University of Oklahoma Press, 1979.

———*Fighting Men of the Indian Wars*. Stillwater, Oklahoma: Barbed Wire Press, 1991.

———*War in East Texas: Regulators vs. Moderators*. Lufkin, Texas: Best of East Texas Publishers, 2006.

Parsons, Chuck. *Sutton-Taylor Feud: The Deadliest Blood Feud in Texas*. Denton: University of North Texas Press, 2009.

Post, Texas: The Gateway to the Plains. Lubbock, Texas: Press of the Plains, 1986.

Post City Centennial Magazine, June 1–3, 2007.

Pritchett, Jewell G., and Erma Barfoot Black. *Kent County and Its People*. Rotan, Texas: Rotan Advance Newspaper Office, 1983.

Scurry County Book Committee. *Footprints Across Scurry County, 1884–1984*. Lubbock: Craftsman Printers, Inc., 1984.

Shakespeare, William. *Romeo and Juliet*, 1597.

Shelton, Gene. *Manhunter: The Life and Times of Frank Hamer*. New York: Berkley Publishing Group, 1997.

Shelton, Hooper, comp. *From Buffalo to Oil: History of Scurry County, Texas*. Snyder, Texas: Feather Press, 1973.

Smallwood, James M. *The Feud That Wasn't*. College Station: Texas A&M Press, 2008.

Sonnichsen, C. L. *I'll Die Before I'll Run*. New York: Devin-Adair Company, 1962.

———*Ten Texas Feuds*. Albuquerque: University of New Mexico Press, 1957.

Sparks, John. "A Winner of the West," *Frontier Times* 16, no. 7 (April 1939).

Stokes, Katy. *Paisano: Story of a Cowboy and A Camp Meeting*. Waco, Texas: Texian Press, 1980.

Tyler, Ron, ed.-in-chief. *The New Handbook of Texas*. 6 vols. Austin: Texas State Historical Association, 1996.

Webb, Walter P. *The Texas Rangers*. Austin: University of Texas Press, 1935.

Yelderman, Pauline. *The Jay Bird Democratic Association of Fort Bend County*. Waco, Texas: Texian Press, 1979.

DVD

Hamer Brothers: Texas Rangers. Written and narrated by Harrison F. Hamer. Tornado Alley Films, 2007.

Index

Note: Page numbers in *italics* refer to illustrations.

C

H

K